BOAS & PYTHONS
AND OTHER FRIENDLY SNAKES
BY JOHN COBORN

BOAS & PYTHONS
AND OTHER FRIENDLY SNAKES
BY JOHN COBORN

1995 Edition

987654321   956789

Distributed in the UNITED STATES to the Pet Trade by T.F.H. Publications, Inc., One T.F.H. Plaza, Neptune City, NJ 07753; distributed in the UNITED STATES to the Bookstore and Library Trade by National Book Network, Inc. 4720 Boston Way, Lanham MD 20706; in CANADA to the Pet Trade by H & L Pet Supplies Inc., 27 Kingston Crescent, Kitchener, Ontario N2B 2T6; Rolf C. Hagen Ltd., 3225 Sartelon Street, Montreal 382 Quebec; in CANADA to the Book Trade by Vanwell Publishing Ltd., 1 Northrup Crescent, St. Catharines, Ontario L2M 6P5 ; in ENGLAND by T.F.H. Publications, PO Box 15, Waterlooville PO7 6BQ; in AUSTRALIA AND THE SOUTH PACIFIC by T.F.H. (Australia), Pty. Ltd., Box 149, Brookvale 2100 N.S.W., Australia; in NEW ZEALAND by Brooklands Aquarium Ltd. 5 McGiven Drive, New Plymouth, RD1 New Zealand; in Japan by T.F.H. Publications, Japan—Jiro Tsuda, 10-12-3 Ohjidai, Sakura, Chiba 285, Japan; in SOUTH AFRICA by Lopis (Pty) Ltd., P.O. Box 39127, Booysens, 2016, Johannesburg, South Africa. Published by T.F.H. Publications, Inc.
MANUFACTURED IN THE UNITED STATES OF AMERICA
BY T.F.H. PUBLICATIONS, INC.

TABLE OF CONTENTS

Introduction

Since the civilization of the human race began (however one cares to interpret this) man has shown an interest in his fellow creatures, and animals of many kinds have been kept in captivity over the centuries. He kept most of these, of course, purely for economic purposes (i.e., to provide meat, milk, or eggs) so it became less necessary to go hunting whenever he was hungry. As time went on, he began to realize the beneficial effects of having certain animals as guards or companions (dogs and cats, for example) and others as purely esthetic or pleasurable additions to the household (cage birds and goldfish, for instance). In the last century or so, however, a thirst for knowledge of the habits of ever more exotic and bizarre creatures has led man to keeping the most unusual household "pets."

While it can be said that the very thought of snakes will terrify most people and many others are largely indifferent to them (unless one comes into their lives), there is a dedicated band of serpent enthusiasts who find great pleasure in studying, keeping, and breeding these fascinating reptiles. A great amount of folklore and tall stories exists about many snake species. Most of these accounts can be dismissed as downright ridiculous, while others may be loosely based on fact. Such stories have stirred the interest of many people with an enquiring mind, and most of our knowledge of the biology of many species is a result of amateur discoveries.

The family of pythons and boas, Boidae, includes among its 90 or so members six of the world's largest serpents. Of these, the Reticulated Python of Southeast Asia has been known to reach a length of 10 meters (33 feet), while the South American Anaconda does not lag far behind; what it

The Green Tree Python of New Guinea, *Chondropython viridis*, is one of the many spectacular species of Boidae. Like many other pythons, however, it is a species for the experienced keeper, not the neophyte. Photo: B. Kahl.

Above and facing page: The longest snake in the world is a python, the Reticulated Python *(Python reticulatus)*. At a common length of 18-20 feet (over 6 meters), it is perhaps the most dangerous non-venomous snake. Young specimens often are available as pets, however. Photo above by S. Kochetov; facing page: P. J. Stafford.

may lack in length it certainly compensates for in weight, being a much more heavily built snake. Not all pythons and boas are particularly large, however, and some species barely reach 60 cm (2 ft) total adult length. Most of the species will settle well into captivity and will become tame and trusting providing they are handled regularly. Many of the species now are bred regularly in captivity, and newly hatched specimens are the best to obtain for taming purposes.

Because many species have suffered seriously at the hands of unscrupulous international animal dealers and from loss of habitat, wild stocks in some areas have been reduced to the point of extinction. Many

countries now have introduced legislation to protect many of the endangered species, and the legitimate pet trade has to rely on captive-bred specimens and imports of only those species still sufficiently common in the wild to not yet warrant protection.

Keeping pythons and

reptiles themselves are clean, odor-free, quiet, and nondemanding given a few simple requirements. After setting up your terrarium and obtaining specimens, cleaning chores and expenses are minimal, and you have a chance of doing your own natural history research.

Anacondas, *Eunectes murinus*, are the most massive snakes, with many records nearing 30 feet (9 meters) and unaccepted records to 37.5 feet (11 meters). This is the most aquatic boa. Photo: M. Freiberg.

boas in the home is a fascinating hobby and has its advantages in comparison to some of the more commonly kept pets. Relatively little space is required, depending on what species are being kept (there is a "size" to suit everybody). Accommodations for snakes can be esthetically pleasing—even attractive—and the

This book has been written with the beginner in mind, but it is hoped that some of the data given will also be useful to more advanced herpetologists or even to those with just a general interest in natural history. It supplies all the information necessary to keep, maintain, and breed one or more of the many species of boids suitable for the home enthusiast.

Natural History of Snakes

   This chapter is intended
to provide basic accounts
of the evolution,
classification, and biology
of snakes in general
and to compare them with
other members of the
class Reptilia as well as
other vertebrate classes.
By having a basic
knowledge of these
various facts, one will
develop a better
understanding of the

Specialty boas and pythons, such as the Australian Diamond Python, *Morelia spilotes*, are expensive and most often available as captive-bred specimens. Photo: C. Banks.

"The word herpetology is derived from the Greek word *herpeton*, which means 'a creeping thing.'"

natural history of our chosen group of snakes that is important if we are going to successfully keep and breed them.

Snakes are reptiles, and the branch of zoology that deals with this class of animals is known as "herpetology." The word herpetology is derived from the Greek word *herpeton*, which means "a creeping thing." In the early days of zoology all lowly animals such as amphibians and reptiles were lumped together in this group of "creeping things," and the word "herpetology" was coined to encompass all of them.

Although the science of zoological classification has advanced tremendously since those days, we are still left with the word that includes the study of all amphibians and reptiles. This is an enormous subject in itself, and it would seem that it is time that individual researchers in the various branches of herpetology have their own name. A person who studies snakes, for example, could be called an "ophiologist" or a "serpentologist."

EVOLUTION OF REPTILES

The reptiles form a class of vertebrate animals intermediate between the fishes and amphibians on one hand and the higher vertebrates (the birds and the mammals) on the other. Modern reptiles include the crocodilians, the turtles, the lizards, the amphisbaenians, and the snakes—not forgetting the lizard-like Tuatara, a

The New Zealand Tuatara, *Sphenodon punctatus*.

Children's Python, *Python childreni*, is a very variable Australia-New Guinea species. Photo: C. Banks.

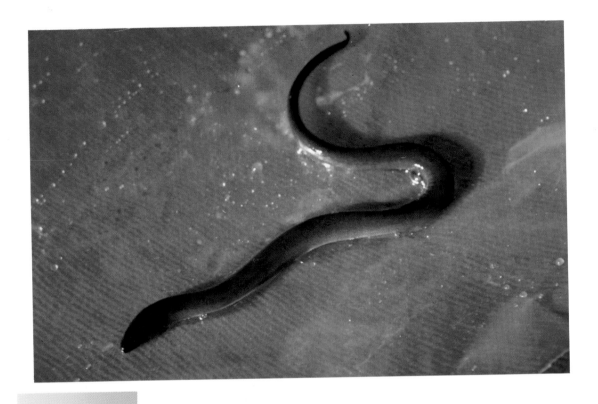

Snake-like animals occur in many groups of vertebrates. This is an *Amphiuma*, a burrowing salamander from the southern United States. A true snake lacks external ear openings, lacks eyelids, lacks legs, has scales, and has a distinctive jaw structure. Photo: Dr. Sherman Minton.

single species that has an order all to itself. Snakes, lizards, and amphisbaenians are closely related and belong to a single order, Squamata, with three suborders.

The ancestors of our modern snakes and lizards appeared along with the first dinosaurs during the late Triassic period, almost 200 million years ago, although fossil records of these reptiles are sparse. The modern lizards (suborder Lacertilia) are likely to have branched off from the primitive order Eosuchia during the Triassic period, but the oldest definite fossil links between modern lizards and their ancestors originated in the Upper Jurassic period, about 140 million years ago. During the same period, the first bird ancestors arose.

It is generally accepted that modern snakes (suborder Serpentes)

millions
of years

millions of years	Period	Events
0	Quarternary	Man
50	Tertiary	grassland formations development of mammals mangrove formation
100	Cretaceous	End of dinosaurs and ammonites Forest formations Angiosperms Snakes
150	Jurassic	Birds Bony fishes Bennettites
200	Triassic	Mammals, dinosaurs, ginkgo Stonecorals
250	Permian	Therapsids Ginkgo and Pelycosaurs Cycas-like conifers
300	Carboniferous	vein-network leaves Original reptiles lepidodendrons seed-ferns
350	Devonian	Quadrupeds (amphibians) Trees Insects (cockroaches) Ammonites
400	Silurian	Original land plants Reefs
450	Ordovician	Limestone algae Vertebrates (jawless)
500	Cambrian	Corals Burgess fauna Trilobites, Molluscs
550 / 600	Vendian	Brachiopods Ediacara fauna

The Table of Geological Time indicates that the original reptiles occurred during the Carboniferous period about 300 million years ago. Snakes first appeared in the fossil record during the Cretaceous about 100 million years ago.

The Crocodylia, the alligators, crocodiles, and their relatives, are among the most spectacular of the living Reptilia and among the most ancient. Here a juvenile American Alligator, *Alligator mississippiensis,* basks on top of two juvenile Spectacled Caimans, *Caiman crocodilus.*

Lizards, such as the Green Anole to the right and the Common Iguana on the facing page, are the closest living relatives of the snakes and often are hard to tell from snakes. There are many legless lizard species, some of them very common.

"The earliest known fossil creatures resembling snakes are from the lower Cretaceous period some 130 million years ago."

arose from the lizards in the early Cretaceous period, about 130 million years ago, but there is no hard and fast fossil evidence to link the two suborders.

Unfortunately, small lizards and snakes do not make good fossils, as the small, delicate bones tend to break down or become scattered.

Paleontologists (people who study fossils) are continually finding various bones, but without the other parts to go with them their task is extremely difficult. One can compare the paleontologist's task to the hardest of jigsaw puzzles, with many of the key pieces missing. Due to this incomplete fossil evidence, snake evolution is based largely on theory. The earliest known fossil creatures resembling snakes are from the lower Cretaceous period some 130 million years ago. These were short and heavy and had a mixture of lizard and snake characteristics.

Unfortunately, there is no intermediary evidence to link these creatures with modern snakes.

One of the most widely

The turtles are a very ancient group of reptiles that are virtually unchanged since they first appear in the fossil record. This Chicken Turtle, *Deirochelys reticularia,* represents one of the fewer than 250 species of living turtles.

accepted theories is that all snakes evolved from burrowing lizards. Certain primitive lizards would have taken to burrowing into the substrate in order to escape from predators and perhaps to hunt other subterranean creatures (as some modern species still do). This

only vestiges remained, these being just suitable for detecting the difference between light and darkness. The method of burrowing meant that limbs also became dispensable, and all snakes have lost their external limbs (although some have retained limb girdles). External ear

The Blood Python, *Python curtus*, of Indo-China is a relatively docile python but often is hard to feed. Photo: C. Banks.

subterranean existence, over countless generations, would mean that certain modifications to the body would be necessary for the animal to remain successful. In the dark, subterranean world, eyes were of little use, so they gradually became absorbed until

openings would have also been an encumbrance in a subterranean environment, so these were also lost.

At a further stage of their evolution, some of these burrowing creatures found it convenient to return to the surface. In a lighter

"In the dark, subterranean world, eyes were of little use."

situation, eyes again became important so they were redeveloped (although the eyelids were completely lost, the eyes being under a transparent protective scale called a brille). The limbs were almost completely or completely lost, so the reptile developed a serpentine method of locomotion. External ear openings were also lost, but modern snakes have developed an efficient mechanism for detecting vibrations through solid surfaces.

Additional adaptations that probably developed during the burrowing period include a sophisticated method of scenting odors and a very highly developed sense of touch. Most modern snakes still have these attributes.

In spite of the theory regarding the evolution of snakes from burrowing lizards, there is no modern lizard family that could be construed to be a

The highly contrasting white labials (lip scales) of the otherwise blackish D'Albert's Python, *Liasis albertisii*, are distinctive. This Australian species is seldom kept by hobbyists. Photo: C. Banks.

The Indian (light phase) Python, *Python molurus molurus*, is an example of a once-common pet species that now is seldom seen in the hobby. India placed it on the protected list, so its importation now is difficult. Photo: S. Kochetov.

link between lizards and snakes. Even the legless amphisbaenians (suborder Amphisbaenia), which were at one time thought to be lizards "turning into snakes," have now been classified into their own suborder. Although they have some characteristics similar to some found in both lizards and snakes, they have further unique characteristics that suggest separate evolution. If the burrowing theory is true, it can only be proved if

and when complete fossils of the intermediate forms are found.

SNAKE CLASSIFICATION

Classification is the means by which we categorize the infinite numbers of animal and plant species found on this planet. Without a logical system of classification, our biological knowledge of almost countless organisms would be in a most untidy state to say the least. Our present

method of classification is based on the work of the Swedish botanist Carl von Linne, generally known as Linnaeus (1707-1778). He devised a system called the "binomial system of nomenclature" in which every kind of animal and plant is given a double name, the first part being that of the genus, the second that of the species. For international communication purposes Latin was the major language used by scientists at the time, and it is therefore not surprising that Linnaeus used this language as a basis for his system, although a fair amount of Greek and a smattering of other languages have also found their way into it.

As an example, the Indian Python has the scientific name of *Python*

Unlike its close relative the Burmese Python, *P. m. bivittatus*, the Indian Python lacks a complete dark arrowhead marking on top of the head. *Python molurus* is perhaps the most desirable and docile of all the pythons kept in captivity. Photo: Cotswold Wildlife Park.

This spectacular specimen of the Burmese Python, *P. m. bivittatus,* shows its distinctive head markings. This is the snake commonly used by snake dancers and seen in carnivals. Photo: B. Kahl.

"In some cases a subspecific name may be added to the binomial, making it a trinomial."

molurus, Python being the genus and *molurus* being the specific part of the name. As there are other types of python in the genus, these are given different specific names (for example: *Python reticulatus, Python sebae,* etc.). In some cases a subspecific name may be added to the binomial, making it a trinomial. This is the case when two geographical races of a species are different, but not different enough to warrant separate species classification. For example, the Indian Python comes in two different geographical races sometimes referred to as the "light phase" and the "dark phase." The former is the true Indian Python and the typical or nominate subspecies, so it is named *Python molurus molurus.* The latter (sometimes referred to as the Burmese Python) is an eastern race or subspecies that has been given the subspecific name of *Python molurus bivittatus.*

For further classification, species are

arranged in genera, genera in families, families in orders, orders in classes, and so on, in ascending order, based on differences and similarities between them. One of the most convenient ways of illustrating the classification of a particular species is to refer to a table. The following table shows as an example the classification of the Indian Python.

Because it is so commonly kept, the Burmese Python often is bred in captivity, making it even more available to hobbyists with the facilities and experience to take care of it. Even albino specimens now are available. Photo above: B. Kahl; below: M. J. Cox.

SNAKE   CLASSIFICATION
(example: Indian Python)

Class:	Reptilia	All Reptiles
Order:	Squamata	Lizards and Snakes
Suborder:	Serpentes	All Snakes
Family:	Boidae	Pythons and Boas
Subfamily:	Pythoninae	All Pythons
Genus:	*Python*	Typical Pythons
Species:	*Python molurus*	Indian Python
Subspecies:	*P. m. molurus*	Light Phase Indian Python
Subspecies:	*P. m. bivittatus*	Dark Phase Indian or Burmese Python.

In normal text, scientific names (genus, species, and subspecies only) are usually printed in italic script. When no italics are available, the names are customarily underlined. It is quite in order to abbreviate a binomial (or a subspecific trinomial) once it has been mentioned in full in the text. For example: *Python molurus bivittatus* can be abbreviated to *P. m. bivittatus.*

There are four orders in the modern class Reptilia: Chelonia (tortoises and turtles), Crocodylia (crocodiles and alligators), Rhynchocephalia (the Tuatara), and Squamata (lizards, amphisbaenians, and snakes). Snakes therefore form a suborder (Serpentes) of the reptiles, sharing the order Squamata with the lizards (Lacertilia) and the amphisbaenians (Amphisbaenia). There are about 3000 species of modern snakes arranged in some 11 families and 354 genera. These figures are only approximate as there are always disagreements among taxonomists (those who study the classification of organisms) when it comes to borderline cases, such as what species belongs to which genus, etc. This is particularly the case with species that closely resemble others. In the following table, a simplified classification of the snake families is given.

In the table, the snake families have been placed in their theoretical order of evolution. The blind snakes are considered to be the most primitive, while the venomous snakes are the most highly developed. It can be seen that the family Boidae is somewhere

"The blind snakes are considered to be the most primitive."

Snake Families	Approx. Number of Genera	Approx. Number of Species
1) Typhlopidae (Blind Snakes)	5	200
2) Leptotyphlopidae (Thread Snakes)	2	50
3) Aniliidae (Cylinder Snakes)	3	9
4) Uropeltidae (Shield-tails)	8	40
5) Boidae (Pythons and Boas)	22	90
6) Xenopeltidae (Sunbeam Snake)	1	1
7) Acrochordidae (Wart Snakes)	2	3
8) Colubridae (Typical Snakes)	250	2500
9) Elapidae (Cobras, Mambas, etc.)	41	180
10) Hydrophiidae (Sea Snakes)	16	50
11) Viperidae (Vipers and Pit Vipers)	14	150

A simplified arrangement of the families of snakes. Other specialists may recognize more families, breaking up the families Boidae and Colubridae into smaller familes.

A Blind Snake of the family Leptotyphlopidae, *Leptotyphlops humilis* of the southwestern United States and Mexico. Photo: K. Lucas, Steinhart Aquarium.

"No other class of vertebrates possesses the combination of all of these three attributes."

near the middle of the evolutionary scale, so pythons and boas, although not as primitive as the blind snakes, are not as highly developed as the colubrids and the venomous snakes.

SNAKE BIOLOGY

It is generally recognized that there are six classes of vertebrate animals, the most advanced (in evolutionary terms) being the Mammalia (mammals), followed by Aves (birds), Reptilia (reptiles), Amphibia (amphibians), Osteichthyes (bony fishes) and Chondrichthyes (cartilaginous fishes). Snakes, being reptiles, are therefore contained somewhere near the middle of the evolutionary scale in the subphylum Craniata (vertebrates). All reptiles possess certain combinations of anatomical, morphological, and behavioral characteristics unique to themselves, making them different from all other vertebrate groups. The simplest recognizable characteristics of reptiles are that they have a scaly skin, they respire by means of lungs, and they are poikilothermic ("cold-blooded," relying on environmental conditions such as sunlight in order to control their body temperatures). No other class of vertebrates possesses the combination of all of these three attributes. Fishes may have a scaly skin and be poikilothermic, but they do not possess conventional lungs; birds may have scales on their legs and possess lungs, but they are homoiothermic ("warm-blooded," with a constant normal body temperature controlled by internal metabolism); amphibians may have lungs, but they do not have a scaly skin; mammals are neither scaly-skinned nor poikilothermic.

In spite of the apparent disadvantage of being poikilothermic, reptiles are able to control their body temperature to a certain extent by a process known as "thermoregulation." They do this by moving in or out of the sun or other warm places, by flattening their bodies, and by using various appendages to gain maximum warmth from the sun's rays. In

"Reptiles are able to control their body temperature to a certain extent by a process known as 'thermoregulation.' "

Some Blind Snakes have distinctive patterns, like this South American *Leptotyphlops weyrauchi,* but most are just shades of brown or black. Photo: S. Holley.

This female Reticulated Python produces heat to help incubate her eggs. The heat results from numerous minor muscular "twitches." Photo: W. B. Allen, Jr.

the development of the embryo (oviparity), or the embryo develops to full-term in the egg within the maternal body and is laid at the point of hatching (ovoviviparity).

Most reptiles are carnivorous, taking prey compatible with their size, but some Chelonia and a few lizard species are wholly or partly herbivorous. Due to their low metabolic rate, reptiles do not require the relatively larger amounts of food necessary to the homoiotherms, and they can only catch and properly digest food when environmental temperatures permit. Reptiles increase in size and range of species as one approaches the tropics, because the climates in these regions allow activity for most of the year. In contrast, the temperate regions contain fewer species that are relatively small and are forced to hibernate during the winter months. Most species of pythons and boas come from the tropics, however, and do not require long periods in hibernation.

general, it can be said that reptiles have a great dependance on thermoregulation, and this is a major factor when designing captive housing.

In the reptiles, fertilization is internal and sperm is passed directly into the ovaries of the female during sexual copulation. The usually shell-covered egg develops to a certain stage in the female's ovaries and is then laid in a warm place where the sun's rays can further aid

In spite of the limits of environmental preferences, snakes have managed to colonize a remarkably high percentage of the earth's surface; they are only completely absent from areas of high latitude and altitude, where the presence of permafrost precludes the opportunity of frost-free hibernation. Even so, a few species manage to survive near, if not within, the Arctic Circle (for example: *Vipera berus*, the European Common Adder, and *Thamnophis sirtalis*, the American Common Garter Snake), while in the Southern Hemisphere *Bothrops ammodytoides*, an Argentine pit viper, is found as far south as latitude 50°. Such cold-climate snakes are active

"A few species manage to survive near, if not within, the Arctic Circle."

This mating pair of Green Tree Pythons, *Chondropython viridis,* is typical of most boids in that the male (head on top) is smaller and more slender than the female, which tends to have a heavier body to accommodate the eggs or young. The cloacas are in contact, with one of the male's hemipenes inserted into the female's cloaca. Photo: C. Banks.

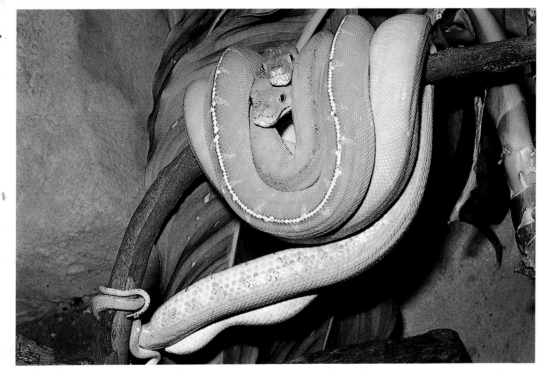

"In the boids, for example, the left lung usually is reduced or absent, only the right lung being fully functional."

for only three or four months of the year, and it is remarkable that such species are able to complete ongoing life cycles in these unlikely environments. The winter months are spent in a state of torpor in a frost-free refuge, usually well below the surface of the ground in a burrow or crevice. Some snakes have even taken to the oceans.

In spite of its long cylindrical shape, a snake possesses all of the essential internal organs that mammals have, but of course they are modified to fit into the narrower space. In the boids, for example, the left lung usually is reduced or absent, only the right lung being fully functional. Looking at the exterior of a typical snake, we will see that there is a head that usually is fairly distinct from the body, a narrower neck running into the body, and, finally, a tail. The body is covered with dry, overlapping scales arranged somewhat in the manner of tiles on a roof. Most boids have smooth, glossy scales, but in some species these may have a dull finish. Colors vary from species to species, and in most cases, including all of the boids, the function is camouflage to help the snake hide from predators and to confuse its own prey.

Perhaps the most obvious point about all snakes is that they are limbless, although some of the more primitive families possess a vestigial pelvic girdle, an indication of evolution from limbed reptiles. The pythons and boas possess such a pelvic girdle and, in addition, the vestiges of the hind limbs appear as "spurs" on either side of the cloaca. In most non-burrowing and non-aquatic species the ventral scales are many times larger and broader than those on the rest of the body. The belly often has a single row of these broad scales that play an important part in the locomotion of terrestrial and arboreal species.

Juvenile Boa Constrictors under about 18 inches (45 cm) often have heavy loads of parasites and lung infections. Many die soon after purchase. Boas over 3 feet (1 m) often are aggressive, however, Photo by B. Kahl.

Snake locomotion is a complex and interesting subject. The method of movement can take several forms. Most of the boids use a combination of "snaking" and "rectilinear crawling" to move from one spot to the next. When snaking, the reptile advances by making a series of lateral curving movements with its body and uses leverage from any kind of solid irregularities in the surface, such as stones, tufts of grass, branches, bark, etc. Rectilinear crawling is used mainly by large snakes when moving slowly. The snake's grip on the surface over which it is moving is provided by the broad, flat ventral scales and, through a complicated system of longitudinal muscle contractions, the snake "walks" on its jointed ribs that push the snake along the ground via the ventral scales. The speed of snakes is often a subject of extreme exaggeration, probably stemming from the fact that most snakes are seen only briefly as they disappear rapidly into the undergrowth. Various experiments have proved that no snake is capable of outpacing a

The taxonomy of many pythons and boas is very confused as they are variable animals. For instance, this Australian python has been called both *Python childreni* and *P. stimsoni*. Photo: C. Banks.

Some boas have large numbers of subspecies, especially those that inhabit different islands. The Caribbean *Epicrates striatus,* for instance, has at least eight subspecies distinguishable by relatively minor differences in pattern and scale counts. Photo: S. Kochetov.

running man on an obstacle-free area.

All snake species are carnivorous and will not take vegetable matter unless by accident (not including that contained in the gut of the prey). It seems that the snake's digestive juices are unable to deal with certain kinds of vegetable matter. A python that consumes a corn-fed chicken, for example, will usually pass the undigested corn out in its feces.

Small snakes will take various kinds of invertebrates, while larger snakes will devour mammals, birds and their eggs, amphibians, and fishes of a size that they can easily overpower. Certain snake species specialize in their choice of food items. There are egg-eating snakes, bird-

The venomous cobras, such as this golden phase Indian or Spitting Cobra, *Naja naja,* are rightly feared, but their venom is an adaptation for killing prey, not attacking humans. No boa or python is venomous, but large species can inflict serious bites that can be slow to heal. Photo: M. J. Cox.

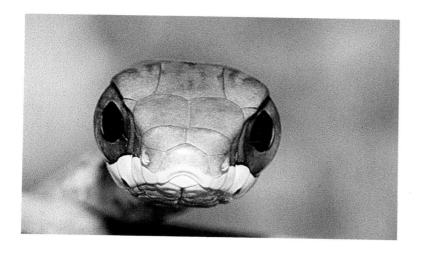

The beautiful green eyes of this juvenile Boomslang, *Dispholidus typus,* are elongated anteriorly, giving the snake some degree of binocular vision useful in hunting birds and lizards. Photo: Dr. G. Dingerkus.

eating snakes, frog-eating snakes, fish-eating snakes, snail-eating snakes, and even snake-eating snakes (the King Cobra, *Ophiophagus hannah,* for example). Pythons and boas are not particularly specialized with regard to their selection of prey. Most of them seem to prefer "warm-blooded" prey (mammals and/or birds), but some will take fishes and other reptiles. Among the boids, however, there are a few species that specialize in certain groups of prey related to their habitat.

All snakes have a highly mobile, two-pronged forked tongue that during times of activity is continually flickering out and in through an opening (labial aperture) at the front of the mouth. The tips of the tongue pick up scent particles from the air or from solid objects and convey them to the palate, where there is a pair of highly developed sensing organs known as the Organs of Jacobson. These vomeronasal organs are literally for smelling the contents of the mouth, and in snakes the tips of the tongue can be inserted into them. The organs correspond to the nostrils but form separate chambers lined with extremely sensitive tissue. This makes snakes extremely efficient scent-oriented animals. Their sense of smell is their most important one and aids them in finding prey, finding water, finding mates, and testing refuges

"Pythons and boas are not particularly specialized with regard to their selection of prey."

Mice of various sizes are perhaps the preferred food of most snakes often kept in captivity. This Rhinoceros Viper, *Bitis nasicornis,* is able to feed on adult mice. Almost all boas and pythons will take mice and rats, until they grow too large to consider such "finger food." Photo: W. B. Allen, Jr.

Facing page: The Green Mamba, *Dendroaspis angusticeps,* is a member of the family Elapidae. This relative of the cobras is considered to be one of the most dangerous African snakes, even though it has relatively small venom fangs.

and egg-laying sites.

Snakes have various means of catching and overpowering their prey, from simply grabbing and swallowing to envenomation. Three families of snakes—the Elapidae (cobras, mambas, etc.), the Hydrophiidae (sea snakes), and the Viperidae (vipers and pit vipers)—are "front-fanged" in that they possess a pair of hypodermic-needle-like fangs at the front of the upper jaw. When prey is bitten the snake injects venom into it via the hollow fangs from a pair of venom sacs, one situated on either side of the head under the skin behind the eye. Such venom is usually sufficient to kill or severely immobilize the prey in a very short period, after which it is devoured in the normal snake way. The large family of snakes known as the Colubridae contains a

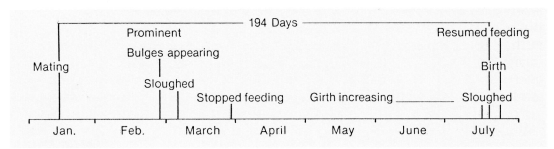

Top: A Boomslang killing a large chameleon. Next to small mammals and birds, lizards are perhaps the most common prey of snakes. Bottom: Diagrammatic record of gestation in a female Cook's Tree Boa, *Corallus enydris.*

"Venomous snakes form only about 10% of the total number of snake species."

relatively small number of species that are also venomous, although in this case they are "rear-fanged," the poorly developed, grooved venom fangs being situated toward the rear of the upper jaw. Such snakes have to "chew" at their victims to get maximum effect from their venom.

Venomous snakes form only about 10% of the total number of snake species, and of these 10% only a few of them can be considered really dangerous to humans. Even so, snakes rarely attack man unless provoked. The majority of fatal snake bites occur in countries where agriculture is primitive and the natives go poorly shod. Another high-risk group is herpetologists!

One good attribute of pythons and boas is that none of them is venomous. They kill their prey by constriction. The advantage of constriction is that the reptiles are able to catch and overpower large prey animals and thus have to feed less frequently. There are many dubious stories going around about large constrictors catching and swallowing animals as large as cattle, even elephants, but it would seem these are mainly folktales. However, a large Reticulated Python or an Anaconda would be quite capable of catching and swallowing a medium-sized deer, antelope, or pig. There are a few authentic reports of the former reptile overpowering and swallowing humans (usually children).

A prey-catching sequence in the life of a boid could be described as follows: The snake would be attracted to the prey first by its movement (most boids are nocturnal and have vertical pupils, a characteristic of many night-active creatures) or (in some species) by the detection of heat from warm-blooded prey. Some species of boids have "heat-sensor pits" arranged in the labial scales around the lips. These are highly efficient in enabling the snake to detect prey, locate it, and judge its distance. As soon as the snake has detected prey in these ways it will become somewhat excited, raising its head and increasing its tongue flickering. At this point, the Organs of

"A large Reticulated Python or an Anaconda would be quite capable of catching and swallowing a medium-sized deer, antelope, or pig."

An excited snake may "stand erect" to better sense its environment, much as this Spectacled Cobra, *Naja naja kaouthia,* is doing. Photo: M. J. Cox.

"Moving the front third of its body into an S-shape, the snake launches its head forward while simultaneously opening its mouth and grabbing the prey."

Jacobson will come into play and further inform the snake of the suitability of the prey item.

Having located the prey and pinpointed its exact position by a combination of sight, odor, and (in appropriate cases) heat reception, the snake will slowly stalk the prey and move itself into a convenient position for striking. Most arboreal boids like to anchor themselves with the tail to a branch before striking, although if the going gets tough with the prey they are not averse to falling off; once the prey is grabbed, the most important thing is to hang on to it, and other considerations are merely secondary!

Moving the front third of its body into an S-shape, the snake launches its head forward while simultaneously opening its mouth and grabbing the prey. The prey may be grabbed at almost any part of its body, but the snake's numerous recurved teeth prevent it from escaping. As soon as the prey is gripped in the mouth the snake will throw several coils of its

The highly flexible body of snakes, such as this Indian Cobra, *Naja naja,* allows them to arch and raise at least the front third of the body for most effective strikes as well as raising the head for a better appreciation of their environment.

body around it and squeeze hard with its strong muscles. In spite of common belief, the prey usually is not "crushed"; just enough pressure is applied to prevent the animal from respiring and possibly also to stop its heartbeat. The prey suffocates in a very short period. When grabbing potentially dangerous (to the snake) prey that would be capable of giving the snake a vicious bite, the snake uses its efficient sense of touch and its coils to maneuver the animal's head into such a position that it is incapable of biting, quite often releasing the grip with the mouth while doing this. As soon as the prey is dead, the snake will begin to examine it carefully, using its tongue to locate the head. Prey is usually swallowed head-first, this being the easiest way of getting it down the gullet.

Snakes are well known for being able to swallow prey several times larger than their own heads. They have several adaptations that enable them to do this. Firstly, the lower jaw is not hinged rigidly to the skull as in most other vertebrates, but is attached by strong, elastic ligaments that allow a

Pythons such as this Australian Carpet Python, *Morelia spilotes,* are able to exert great amounts of force when constricting prey, but they seldom break bones as commonly believed. Constricting prevents rib movement and thus breathing, so prey suffocates. Photo: C. Banks.

"Snakes are well known for being able to swallow prey several times larger than their own heads."

Almost all snakes can swim, the long intestine providing buoyancy and the flexible musculature allowing side-to-side swimming movements.

Photo of *Dispholidus typus,* the Boomslang.

"After taking a heavy meal a boid becomes lethargic and may take a week or more to digest the prey."

huge gape when the jaw is virtually "unhinged." Secondly, the fronts of the lower jaws are also connected with elastic tissue, allowing an enormous spread and also enabling the left and right jaw to work independently of each other. Thirdly, the brain case is tough, totally enclosed, and movable, so it cannot be easily damaged. Fourthly, the tissues of the gut, the flesh, and the skin are highly elastic to enable large prey to be accommodated.

Having gotten to the snout of the prey animal (boids often hold the prey in the coils until after they start to swallow it), the snake opens its mouth and begins to swallow. If you watch this process, the snake actually appears to be moving over the prey animal, working one side of the jaw and then the other as the food slowly disappears into the gullet. After the prey has been forced through the relatively narrow neck region, it is moved more speedily into the stomach by the peristaltic action of the muscles.

After taking a heavy meal a boid becomes lethargic and may take a week or more to digest the prey. During this time the snake is at its most vulnerable, and it will attempt to get into some kind of cover and rely on its camouflage to protect it. Most of the very large species are not susceptible to attack by predators, but smaller species usually live and hunt under cover. Some species partially submerge in water or mud at this time, while others live in burrows below the substrate.

All snakes shed their skins in a process known as "molting" or "sloughing." The regularity and frequency with which this occurs is affected by such things as diet, growth, and climate. Young snakes shed more frequently than older ones as they are growing at a faster rate. All snakes grow throughout their lives, but the rate of growth diminishes with age.

The old, worn skin is pushed away from the newly formed skin beneath by the release of a special fluid. A couple of days before sloughing occurs, the old skin takes on a dull appearance and a milky clouding will be seen in the eyes. This "blue eye" condition is the result of the sloughing

Snakes have a fascination for small children, especially if they are taught correct handling and safety procedures. The species of snake must be carefully chosen for its docility, and adults should always be present to supervise each encounter. Photo: S. C. Miller.

Corallus enydris cookii, Cook's Tree Boa. This is a newborn. Photo by P. J. Stafford.

fluid being present between the old and the new spectacles or brilles (which are, in effect, part of the skin). About a day before sloughing starts the snake becomes restless and the milky appearance in the eyes disappears. By rubbing the lips on rough objects such as bark or stones, the snake will loosen the skin at the edges and will eventually crawl out of the old skin. In a healthy snake the skin turns inside out and peels off much in the manner of a lady removing her stocking. The new skin is full of color and sheen, and a freshly shed snake is at its most beautiful. It will most likely feed shortly after sloughing (most snakes do not feed for at least a week prior to shedding).

ECOLOGY AND CONSERVATION OF THE BOIDAE

Ecology is the interaction of animals and plants with each other and the environment in which they live. It is a complex and fascinating subject. Ecology is a modern

"Ecology is the interaction of animals and plants with each other and the environment in which they live."

Even the dullest snake colors come to life after a molt. The loss of the old dead, almost opaque, skin allows the oily sheens of the freshly exposed skin to dominate. Photo: *Natrix maura*, B. Kahl.

"The larger boids in particular are unable to continue to inhabit areas that have been extremely developed."

Sea snakes are perhaps the most distinctive of the living snakes, their special adaptations allowing them to even feed and breed under water, most species being unable to function on land. Photo: D. Reed.

natural history discipline that is very much in fashion at the present time. By studying ecology, scientists can discover ways of preserving wildlife that would otherwise become extinct. The biggest destroyer of natural ecologies is man himself. Commercial exploitation of natural habitats for industrial, agricultural, and residental purposes will eventually destroy many forms of wildlife with the exception of those species that are able to adapt to new and alien surroundings. Most reptile species are not very adaptable to new

surroundings, and in any case snakes (whether venomous or not) are not tolerated in populated areas. The larger boids in particular are unable to continue to inhabit areas that have been extremely developed. The rate at which natural habitats of many animals are disappearing is much too high, and although many groups and governments are discussing means of wildlife conservation, still not enough is being done to preserve natural habitats. Unfortunately, the economy of most countries dictates that profit is the prior factor before others are taken into consideration. Some

The genus *Laticauda* contains the least modified sea snakes, species still able to function on land. Many taxonomists feel they are actually modified kraits rather than true sea snakes.

countries have set aside national parks in which the terrain will remain in its original condition and in which all indigenous animals and plants are protected. Unfortunately, many of these parks are too small for populations of certain species to be maintained over many generations.

Many studies have been carried out by zoologists on the ecology of various snake species, but there is still a great deal to be learned about those of which we know next to nothing about their biology in the wild.

Captive keeping and breeding of boids can provide us with much information about their behavior, particularly as it is so difficult to study the habits of these secretive creatures in the wild. For this reason it is important to keep a diary on the behavior of any specimens you may keep and to have articles on your experiences published in specialist journals. If you are fortunate enough to live near or are able to visit a place where wild boids occur, you may be able to make a study of your own.

"Captive keeping and breeding of boids can provide us with much information about their behavior."

Facing page: *Laticauda colubrinus,* one of the "false" sea snakes.
Left: Another phase of Children's Python. This form is sometimes called *Python gilbertii,* a species of doubtful validity. Photo: C. Banks.

Take notes, take photographs of the habitat, and record any information you think might be useful. Every species has its own particular ecological niche, and a knowledge of the wild habitat of a species gives one a much better understanding of its requirements in captivity. It is not always possible to visit the location from which your chosen species originated, but there is nothing to stop you from finding out more about the country and its climate. A good quality world atlas is a gold mine of information and should be in the library of every herpetologist. You can study climatic graphs and seasonal variations as well as find out more about local topography.

"A good quality world atlas is a gold mine of information and should be in the library of every herpetolgist."

The "fangs" of this Emerald Tree Boa, *Corallus caninus,* are not for the delivery of a venomous bite. They are long enough to penetrate the feathers of the birds that are the common prey of the species. The long anterior fangs also allow them to give formidable bites. The mouths of large boids are infested with many bacteria, often leading to infected bites that take a long time to heal and may require medication.

A Selection of Species

As there are approximately 90 species of pythons and boas, it would be an impossible task to comprehensively cover all of them in a small book like this. However, I have selected a number of species, based on their availability and suitability as terrarium subjects as well as a few of the rarer species, to

This Emerald Tree Boa clearly shows the labial heat receptors found in some boids. Taxonomists use the degree of development and placement of these labial pits to aid in classification.

"The classification of the boids has posed some difficulties to taxonomists, but it is generally recognized that there are seven subfamilies."

whet the appetites of the ambitious. It is highly recommended that beginners start with those species that are recommended as "easy" before venturing onto more difficult projects.

The classification of the boids has posed some difficulties to taxonomists, but it is generally recognized that there are seven subfamilies: Boinae (typical boas); Bolyerinae (Round Island Boas); Calabarinae (Calabar Ground Python): Erycinae (sand boas, Rubber Boa, and Rosy Boa); Loxoceminae (Mexican Dwarf Boa); Pythoninae (typical pythons); and Tropidophinae (wood snakes or dwarf boas). In the species listings below the maximum lengths given are the longest one would expect to find in any particular species when it is adult. The average adult lengths are usually somewhat shorter.

SUBFAMILY BOINAE— TYPICAL BOAS

This subfamily is very widespread. Although most species occur in Central and South

"All members of the Boinae are ovoviviparous, giving birth to fully developed young."

America, there are another three in Madagascar and three more in New Guinea and other islands in the region. All members of the Boinae are ovoviviparous, giving birth to fully developed young. The genera *Corallus, Epicrates,* and *Sanzinia* possess heat receptors in labial pits; these are situated between the labial scales of the upper lip, rather than within them as is the case with the python species that possess them. There are approximately 26 species in 7 genera.

Corallus caninus
EMERALD TREE BOA
LENGTH: max: 2.5 m (8.1 ft); avg: 1.5 m (5 ft)

An Emerald Tree Boa, *Corallus caninus,* in its very distinctive resting posture. Notice the relatively large scales on the anterior snout, a feature that distinguishes this species from the almost identical Green Tree Python, which has very small scales on the snout. Photo: H. Hansen.

DESCRIPTION: This snake bears an amazing resemblance to the Green Tree Python (*Chondropython viridis*) but belongs to a completely different subfamily. The labial pits are placed between the lip scales, not within them as in the Pythoninae. It is a laterally compressed snake with a broad head and relatively narrow neck. In color it is emerald green with irregular white blotches along the spine; the underside is pale to ochre yellow. Young are orange, acquiring the adult coloration over several years.

RANGE: Tropical South America.

HABITAT AND HABITS: A truly arboreal species of the tropical rain forests, it rarely descends to the ground and should it do so accidentally it can move only awkwardly. At rest this species (like *Chondropython viridis*) has

A close-up of the cloacal (vent) region of an Emerald Tree Boa. Clearly shown are the wide ventral scales or scutes, the anal plate actually covering the vent, the cloacal spurs, and the single row of wide subcaudal scales or scutes. Photo: S. Kochetov.

The Emerald Tree Boa on this page at first glance appears identical with the unrelated Green Tree Python (from New Guinea) on the facing page. Although unrelated at the subfamily level, superficially the two are alike even in their resting posture. Details of head scalation, however, readily distinguish the two. Photo at right: B. Kahl; facing page: W. Tomey.

"The Emerald Tree Boa requires a large terrarium or tropical greenhouse with plenty of stout horizontal branches on which it can move and rest."

a habit of arranging its coils neatly across a horizontal branch, with the head somewhere near the center. In the wild it feeds on birds, bats, and small arboreal mammals (including small primates). Anchoring itself to a branch with its prehensile tail, it catches and constricts its prey and swallows it while hanging head downward. CAPTIVE CARE: This species requires a large terrarium or tropical greenhouse with plenty of stout horizontal branches on which it can move and rest. As it is a rainforest species, it requires a high humidity. Some provision must be made for robust leafy plants (such as *Ficus* and *Philodendron* species) in the terrarium, over which the snake will drape itself. Daytime temperature may reach 28°C (86°F), which can be reduced to about 22°C (72°F) at night. Maintain a high humidity by regular misting and provide a dish of drinking water; the species rarely immerses itself in water. Use broad-spectrum (daylight) fluorescent tubes for lighting. This species is often difficult to adapt to a captive diet,

but with much patience and coaxing it will eventually readily take dead mice and young chicks.

REPRODUCTION: The Emerald Tree Boa is ovoviviparous, producing, on average, 15-30 young. Rarely bred in captivity. This species is most suitable for the advanced herpetologist.

RELATED SPECIES: The smaller Cook's Tree Boa, *Corallus enydris*, grows to about 1.5 m (5 ft) and is yellowish brown in color. It requires care similar to *C. caninus*.

Boa constrictor

COMMON BOA, BOA CONSTRICTOR

LENGTH: max: 4.2 m (14 ft); avg: 3 m (10 ft)

DESCRIPTION: This species is more subject to exaggeration about its size than any other boid, but it is in fact one of the smaller "giants," coming in about sixth in the world stakes. It is a robust species with a large, triangular head set off from the stout body by a narrower neck. There is great variation in color and pattern throughout the range, but the basic ground color is usually creamy buff, marked with

The Garden Boa, *Corallus annulatus,* the third and least frequently seen species of *Corallus.* Photo: W. B. Allen, Jr.

large, uneven saddles in various shades of brown, these becoming progressively more reddish brown toward the tail. In some specimens the tail markings are almost pure red.
RANGE: Central and South America from Mexico to Argentina.
HABITAT AND HABITS: An extremely adaptable species occurring from rocky semi-desert and scrubland to montane rain forest. In the forest environment it is mainly arboreal but comes to the ground to forage. It is often found near human habitations and is occasionally blamed for stealing chickens. It is mainly nocturnal.
CAPTIVE CARE: Adults require a large terrarium (at least 2 × 1 × 1 m, 6.5 × 3.25 × 3.25 ft) with strong climbing branches and ledges or shelves. A voluminous water bath is

A dark phase Cook's Tree Boa, *Corallus enydris cookii*. This species of boa occurs in many different patterns and colors, some brilliant, others dull. Photo: P. J. Stafford.

> "Adults will live satisfactorily on a diet of rats, rabbits, and medium-sized chickens."

At a common maximum size of between 12 and 14 feet (3 to 4 m), the Boa Constrictor is the most commonly seen giant snake. Many specimens are very docile if treated well from an early age, but like any boid they are not always trustworthy. This species now is being bred more commonly in captivity, and several color varieties are available. Photo on facing page: B. Kahl.

essential. The substrate can consist of large grade gravel. The daytime temperature should be maintained at around 28°C (82°F), but reduced to 20°C (68°F) at night. Humidity should be medium. Adults will live satisfactorily on a diet of rats, rabbits, and medium-

100 days after fertilization. The Boa Constrictor is bred frequently in captivity. Young specimens are recommended for the beginner, as older specimens can become irritable and will bite unless they are constantly handled.

sized chickens. Juveniles can be fed with mice and day-old chicks.
REPRODUCTION: Best kept singly outside the breeding season, introducing the pairs at breeding time. Females produce a brood of 30-50 live young approximately

Epicrates cenchria
RAINBOW BOA
LENGTH: max: 2.1 m (7 ft); avg: 1.45 m (4.5 ft)
DESCRIPTION: This is a short but stout boa with a narrow head. It comes in variable colors but is usually shades of bronze-

brown, lighter on the underside. Most individuals have dark circular markings along the body. The most noteworthy feature of this beautiful species is the bloom of color on the body scales, especially after a recent molt. When viewed in certain angles of light, this bloom shows all the colors of the rainbow, somewhat like a thin film of oil floating on water. Like the genus *Corallus, Epicrates* species possess labial heat receptor pits.

RANGE: Northern and central South America.

HABITAT AND HABITS: Found more in forested areas than in open country; it is fairly arboreal but will come to the ground to forage. Mainly nocturnal, coming into action at dusk.

CAPTIVE CARE: The Rainbow Boa requires a large, tall terrarium suited to its arboreal habits with stout climbing branches and robust plants. An adequate water container is required in which this species will readily and regularly immerse itself. Daytime temperatures should be maintained at 24-28°C (75-82°F), reduced to about 22°C (72°F) at night. A medium to high humidity should be maintained. This species settles well into captivity, becomes exceedingly tame, and rarely bites. It will take mice, small rats, and day-old chicks eagerly.

REPRODUCTION: An ovoviviparous species producing up to 20 live young each about 30 cm (1 ft) in length. The young should be reared on small mice. Its docile disposition makes it ideal for beginners.

Epicrates striatus
HAITIAN BOA
LENGTH: max: 3.5 m (11.4 ft); avg: 3 m (9.75 ft)
DESCRIPTION: This is a long, slender species with the head well set off from the body by a slender neck. The relatively long tail is prehensile. The ground color is copper-brown, and there are narrow whitish, zig-zag, transverse bands along the body. The underside is lighter colored.
RANGE: The island of Hispaniola in the West Indies.

"This species settles well into captivity, becomes exceedingly tame, and rarely bites."

This weakly patterned but very iridescent Rainbow Boa belongs to one of the subspecies in which adults are almost uniformly brown. The oil-like rainbow of colors still makes this a beautiful snake, however. Photo: B. Kahl.

A Rainbow Boa at its best is a beautiful snake indeed. Notice the black and white eye-like markings on the lower sides typical of the subspecies *E. c. cenchria*. Photo: R. S. Simmons.

Epicrates striatus is a very common Caribbean species found in many varieties on several islands. It is known as the Haitian Boa or Fischer's Boa, the latter name after the German herpetolgist who first described the species. Photo: J. Dodd.

HABITAT AND HABITS: A mainly arboreal species of the forests, but it may often be found in cultivated areas, even near human habitations, where it has a good reputation as a rodent catcher. Mainly nocturnal.

CAPTIVE CARE: Requires similar but larger housing than that described for the Rainbow Boa. Daytime temperature to 28°C (82°F), reduced to 20°C (68°F) at night. A large bathing vessel should be provided. Feeds well on mice, rats, and chicks.

REPRODUCTION: Regular captive breeding occurs; this is probably the most prolific of the island *Epicrates* species. The female gives birth to 9-25 live young, averaging about 15. These are usually 35-45 cm (14-18 in) in length and may be reared on small mice.

RELATED SPECIES: There are a number of subspecies and species in the genus *Epicrates*. Many of these are forms found on individual islands of the West Indies. They include *E. angulifer* (Cuban Boa); *E. chrysogaster* (Turks and Caicos Island Boa); *E. exsul* (Abaco Boa); *E. fordii* (Ford's Boa); *E. gracilis* (Haitian Vine Boa); *E. inornatus* (Puerto Rican Boa); *E. subflavus* (Jamaican Boa). Many other island forms are subspecies of the main species. Some are endangered in the wild and may be obtained for captive breeding programs only under

"This is probably the most prolific of the island *Epicrates* species."

"Some are endangered in the wild and may be obtained for captive breeding programs only under license."

Studies of *Epicrates striatus.* Although not a brilliantly colored boa, it is moderately available and a decent pet. Some specimens are nasty, however, but the relatively small size keeps it manageable. Photo to right: C. Banks; below: P. J. Stafford.

Left: Like most other boas, the Haitian Boa feeds well on mice of various sizes. Photo: J. T. Kellnhauser.

Below: *Epicrates fordii,* Ford's Boa, a small species also found on the Caribbean island of Hispaniola. Photo: P. J. Stafford.

The Puerto Rico Boa, *Epicrates inornatus,* is now protected. Island boas often have small populations. Photo: Dr. S. Minton.

The larger Cuban Boa, *Epicrates angulifer,* tends to be found near caves and eats a large number of bats as part of its regular diet. Photo: S. Kochetov.

license. In most cases husbandry is as described for *E. striatus.*

Eunectes murinus
ANACONDA
LENGTH: max: 9 m (29 ft); avg: 5 m (16.5 ft)
DESCRIPTION: The Anaconda is one of the like eyes and the nostrils are set on top of the relatively narrow head, indicating the snake's semi-aquatic habits. There is a dark-bordered yellow stripe running from behind the eye to the back of the head. The smooth body scales are

A juvenile Anaconda, *Eunectes murinus,* shows little of the potential for its truly giant adult size. Probably more tall tales are told about Anacondas than about any other boas. Photo: Dr. G. Dingerkus.

giants of the snake world and is probably the world's heaviest snake; a large specimen may weigh in excess of 150 kg (330 lbs). It is stouter and heavier than the Reticulated Python, which is the world's longest snake. The bead- colored a dull olive-brown to greenish, broken with a number of dark spots and blotches. Along the flanks these blotches are more numerous and are centered with ochre yellow. The underside is yellowish white, flecked with black.

"The Anaconda . . . is probably the world's heaviest snake; a large specimen may weigh in excess of 150 kg (330 lbs)."

RANGE: Tropical rainforest regions of the Amazon and Orinoco basins.

HABITAT AND HABITS: Never found far from water, this species is semi-aquatic, swimming well and often catching prey under water. It will feed on fishes, caimans, water birds, and mammals, including those up to the size of a large capybara. It is also an adept climber and may often bask on strong limbs overhanging the water. Its main activity time is at night.

CAPTIVE CARE: Anyone acquiring Anacondas must have the space and the funds to maintain them when they reach a large size. A large, drainable, heated pool is essential. Strong climbing branches should be provided. A humid atmosphere is required with a 24-hour temperature in the range of 26-28°C (79-82°F). The pool water should be maintained at 24-26°C (75-79°F). Heat lamps should be provided in strategic basking positions so that the snake has the opportunity of warming

This gorgeous small Anaconda is only a few feet long and still small enough to become a pet. However, it soon will grow beyond a size that can be handled by one person. Large Anacondas also are noted for their bad tempers, making it difficult to maintain them in hygienic surroundings. Photo: B. Kahl.

"Anyone acquiring Anacondas must have the space and the funds to maintain them when they reach a large size."

its huge bulk to a preferred temperature. The use of plants in a terrarium for such a heavy species is usually futile unless thick-trunked trees can be provided. Small specimens can be fed on fish, rats, and small chickens; larger specimens need rabbits, chickens, ducks, and geese.

REPRODUCTION: Captive reproduction is normally confined to zoological parks where there is adequate space for large specimens. The young are about 90 cm (3 ft) in length, and there are usually 25-45 in a clutch. Anacondas can be unreliable and give a vicious bite. For this reason they are only recommended for the more advanced herpetologist.

RELATED SPECIES: The Southern Anaconda, *E. notaeus*, from the pampas lands of central South America, is a much smaller species reaching

This view clearly shows the dorsally situated eyes and closable nostrils that allow the Anaconda to become virtually aquatic. Specimens are almost never found far from larger bodies of water. Photo: K. T. Nemuras.

Eunectes notaeus is a smaller version of the Anaconda that is found south of the Amazon Basin. It commonly is called the Yellow Anaconda because of the yellowish background color of many specimens. It is not as aquatic as its larger cousin and is more likely to be found basking on firm ground. Photo at left: B. Kahl; that below: M. Freiberg.

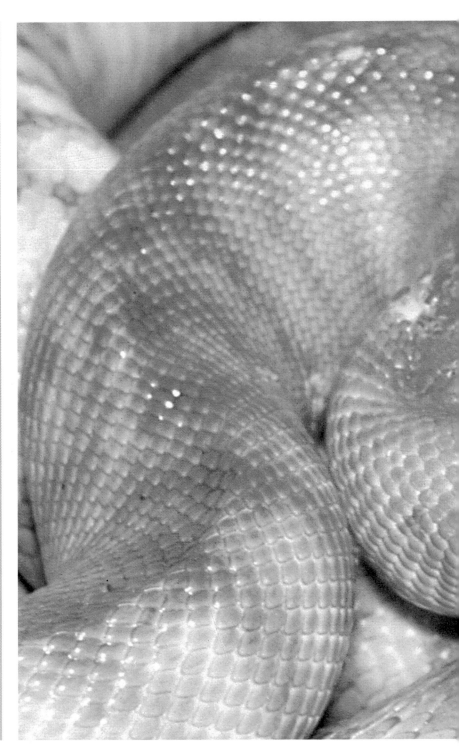

Ramsay's Python, *Aspidites ramsayi*, showing skin damage on the nape. Photo by R. T. Hoser.

These photos show the distinctly flattened head of the Anaconda, with its high eye placement and small nostrils that can be closed by valves to allow long submersion. Photo at right: M. Freiberg; below: Courtesy London Zoo.

a maximum length of 4.5 m (13 ft), most specimens being shorter. It is attractively colored in yellow and black and requires similar but less room than *E. murinus*. In the winter this species can be kept at a slightly lower temperature (max 24°C (75°F), min 16°C (60°F) for four months).

SUBFAMILY BOLYERINAE—ROUND ISLAND BOAS

This subfamily consists of only two species, *Bolyeria multocarinata* and *Casarea dussumieri*, both of which inhabit Round Island, a small island in the Indian Ocean near Mauritius, east of Madagascar. Due to human interference,

including the introduction of feral animals to the island, loss of vegetation and erosion has seriously affected the habitat of these boas and other indigenous animals. The Round Island boas are virtually unique among the Boidae in lacking vestigial pelvic girdles and hind limbs, and are considered to be a possible evolutionary link between the boids and the more advanced colubrids. The jaws have a unique hinging system. It would be a great pity if these species were to become extinct before we know their full evolutionary story. Certain institutions are endeavoring to carry out captive breeding projects,

"The Round Island boas are virtually unique among the Boidae in lacking vestigial pelvic girdles and hind limbs."

The Calabar Ground Python, *Calabaria reinhardtii*, has the heavy-snouted, very polished look typical of burrowers. This small and shy burrower is seldom available and often is difficult to feed in captivity. Photo: P. J. Stafford.

The freckled appearance of the Calabar Ground Python serves as camouflage during the snake's nocturnal above-ground movements. No two specimens are exactly alike in coloration and pattern. Photo: P. J. Stafford.

and one day they may be generally available to the private herpetologist, but at the present time they are unlikely to become available.

SUBFAMILY CALABARINAE— CALABAR GROUND PYTHON

There is only one species in this subfamily. *Calabaria reinhardtii* of West Africa is a small, burrowing boid that reaches a maximum length of 1 m (39 in). The body is more or less the same diameter throughout and is reddish brown in color with lighter spots. The head and the blunt tail are darker brown. This species is rarely kept in captivity and can be described as difficult, as its feeding and breeding habits are poorly understood. It would make a good subject for captive research.

SUBFAMILY ERYCINAE—SAND BOAS

Members of this subfamily occur in both

the Old World (sand boas) and in America (Rubber Boa, Rosy Boa). All members of the subfamily are typically small, rarely reaching 1 m (39 in) in ength. Most of them are terrestrial burrowing species with thick-set cylindrical bodies, a shovel-shaped snout, and a short, blunt tail.

Eryx johnii
INDIAN SAND BOA
LENGTH: max: 85 cm (33 in); avg: 60 cm (24 in)
DESCRIPTION: This species has a typical cylindrical body and a short tail that is the same shape as the head. It is a fairly uniform sandy brown in color, lighter on the underside. Like other members of the subfamily, it will lift

Indian Sand Boas make good pets even for beginners as long as you can provide them with the proper dry environment. They are not very interesting in either appearance or behavior, however, which limits their popularity.
Photo: J. P. Swaak.

This adult Indian Sand Boa shows remnants of the juvenile pattern in the dark bands still faintly visible on the tail. It is not uncommon for all-dark adult snakes to have banded young. Photo: B. Kahl.

and jab with its tail when disturbed and seek a means of burrowing to escape at the head end.

RANGE: Asia Minor to India.

HABITAT AND HABITS: A burrowing species found in steppes, semi-desert, and brushland. It may be active in its subterranean environment at all times of the day or night, and it may come to the surface at night or after heavy rains.

CAPTIVE CARE: Requires a low, desert-type terrarium with a substrate of coarse sand at least 15 cm (6 in) deep. A few flat stones and a dish of drinking water will complete the furnishings. For esthetic purposes, one or two potted succulent plants can be included. Maintain daytime temperature at 30°C (86°F), reduced to about 20°C (68°F) at night. Humidity should be kept low. Feed on mice or lizards.

REPRODUCTION: An ovoviviparous species producing up to 15 live young. These may be reared on new-born mice. This species is recommended for beginners.

RELATED SPECIES: There are several other species

"It may be active in its subterranean environment at all times of the day or night."

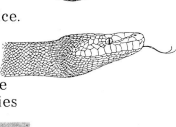

Juveniles of *Eryx johnii* will accept both pink mice and small lizards such as skinks. The dark bands are distinctive at this age but will soon disappear. It is important that the terrarium be dry and relatively warm. Photo: Dr. S. Minton.

Right: A head study of *Eryx johnii*, the Indian Sand Boa. Photo: G. Marcuse.

Below: *Eryx miliaris* is another burrowing boa. It is found in Central Asia, including Mongolia. Like other *Eryx* it requires a warm, dry terrarium. Photo: S. Kochetov.

Left: Although it is called the European Sand Boa, *Eryx jaculus* is actually a species of southwestern Asia that barely crosses the boundaries of eastern Europe. Photo: C. Banks.

Below: *Eryx tataricus*, the Tartar Sand Boa, seldom is found in captivity. When it has been kept, it has not presented any particular problems in its husbandry. Photo: S. Kochetov.

One of the most popular sand boas is the Kenyan Sand Boa, *Eryx colubrinus loveridgei,* of eastern Africa. Few adults are as attractive as this strikingly marked specimen. Photo: L. Porras.

"The Rosy Boa is a sturdily built small boa with a narrow, oval head and a fairly short tail."

in the genus, including the Rough-tailed Sand Boa, *Eryx conicus*; the European Sand Boa, *Eryx jaculus*; and Mueller's Sand Boa, *Eryx muelleri,* all of which require husbandry similar to that for *E. johnii.*

Lichanura roseofusca
ROSY BOA

LENGTH: max: 106 cm (42 in); avg: 80 cm (32 in)

DESCRIPTION: This is a sturdily built small boa with a narrow, oval head and a fairly short tail. It is bluish gray in color with three longitudinal reddish brown to pink broken stripes along the body.

RANGE: Southern California, southwestern Arizona, and northwestern Mexico.

HABITAT AND HABITS: Found in scrubland and open woodland, usually in rocky areas and ravines. Mainly nocturnal and terrestrial, but can climb into low vegetation in search of prey.

CAPTIVE CARE: Requires a medium-sized terrarium with a coarse sand or light gravel substrate mixed with some leaf litter. A climbing branch and one or two robust potted plants can be provided. It requires a shallow water dish with an aquarium heater to provide a medium humidity level. Maintain at a daytime temperature of 28°C (82°F), reduced to 20°C (68°F) at night. Feed on small mice or chicks.

REPRODUCTION: Gives

One of the two native United States boas, the Rosy Boa, *Lichanura roseofusca*, is also quite a good pet. Although a desert species, it does not need high heat and can tolerate a fair amount of humidity. Several distinctive patterns occur in this species, and there is considerable controversy as to the proper names to apply. Photo: I. Francais.

birth to 6-10 live young in late fall after being gravid for about 130 days. Youngsters are about 30 cm (12 in) in length. They may be reared on pink mice.

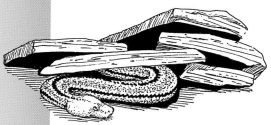

Charina bottae
RUBBER BOA

LENGTH: max: 84 cm (33 in); avg: 50 cm (20 in)

DESCRIPTION: As its common name implies, this species has a rubbery appearance. Its blunt head and tail make it appear to have a head at each end. It is a uniform olive-green to chocolate-brown in color.

RANGE: Western North America from British Columbia to southern California, eastward to Montana, Wyoming, and Utah.

HABITAT AND HABITS: A nocturnal species and an accomplished burrower, living in loose earth, leaf litter, and rotting timber. It can also swim and climb if necessary; it has

a prehensile tail.

GENERAL CARE: Requires a small to medium-sized terrarium with a deep, sandy substrate to enable it to burrow. Decoration can consist of a few flat stones and a couple of potted plants. Keep at a daytime temperature of 30°C (86°F), reduced to 22°C (72°F) at night. Allow a winter rest period at

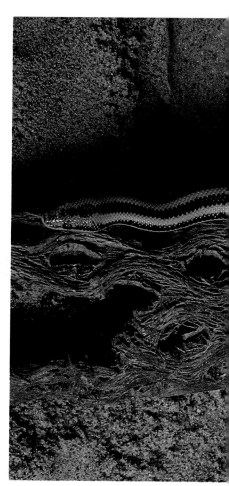

reduced temperatures. Feed on mice.

REPRODUCTION: Ovoviviparous, producing 2-10 young in late summer.

SUBFAMILY LOXOCEMINAE— MEXICAN DWARF BOA

The Mexican Dwarf Boa, *Loxocemus bicolor*, found from western Mexico south to Costa Rica, is the only species in a subfamily that has created many problems for taxonomists. It is now usually recognized as a primitive boa. Little is documented on its habits and reproductive behavior except that it is a burrower. It is bronze-brown in color with a beautiful iridescent sheen.

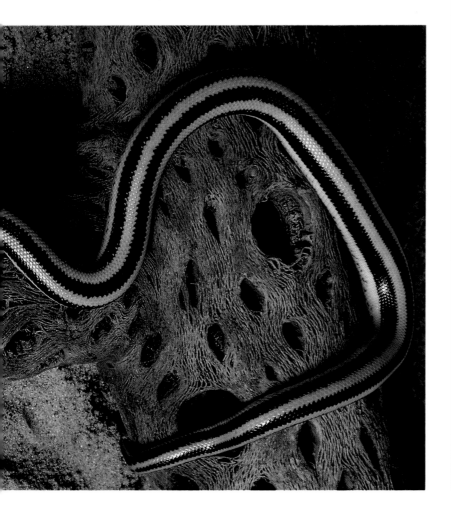

This strongly patterned Rosy Boa has sharply defined dark stripes with little speckling between the stripes. Regardless of pattern, Rosy Boas are rather gentle snakes. Captive-bred specimens are fairly commonly available. Photo: I. Francais.

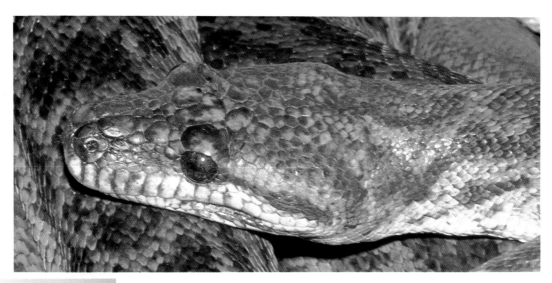

SUBFAMILY PYTHONINAE— TYPICAL PYTHONS

The Pythoninae are confined to the Old World, including Australasia. They include many of the world's longest snakes, including the Reticulated Python (*Python reticulatus*), which may reach 10 m (33 ft) in length. Many python species are a familiar sight in zoo reptile collections, and some are extremely popular with amateur herpetologists.

Pythons are all oviparous, and some of them exhibit parental care in that the female incubates the eggs. All pythons have heat-sensitive labial pits to enable them to detect warm-blooded prey, but unlike the Boinae species that have similar pits, the pits are *within* the labial scales rather than between them.

Python molurus

INDIAN PYTHON
LENGTH: max: 7 m (23 ft); avg: 5 m (16.5 ft)
DESCRIPTION: There are two well documented races, the light phase Indian Python, *P. m. molurus,* and the dark phase Indian or Burmese Python, *P. m. bivittatus.* The latter is the one most often seen in collections. It is a rich bronze-brown in color, marked with a network of broad cream to buff bands bordered with black. There is a complete dark arrow on top of the

head. The former is similarly marked but altogether lighter in color, with an incomplete arrow.

RANGE: India, Sri Lanka, Burma, Indo-China, Malaysia, and western Indonesia.

HABITAT AND HABITS: It prefers forested areas, particularly near water and rocky escarpments. Mainly nocturnal. Climbs and swims well and often submerges in water. It becomes remarkably tame in captivity and is perhaps the most popular of the larger boids.

GENERAL CARE: A young specimen can be kept in a small terrarium, but it will soon outgrow this. Unless you have space for larger terraria you should not start with this species. Females and males should be kept separately outside the breeding season. Each adult snake requires a terrarium at least 2 × 1 × 1 m (6.5 × 1.25 × 1.25 ft), with hefty climbing branches, a shingle substrate, and a deep water bath, preferably with a drain. Daytime temperature should be maintained around 28°C (82°F), reduced by about 5°C (9°F)

at night. Humidity should be medium to high. Try and give dry and humid seasonal variations. Feed small specimens on mice, larger ones on rats, chickens, and rabbits.

REPRODUCTION: This species probably breeds more readily in captivity than any other boid. The female lays 25-60 eggs and coils around them for incubation. The best results occur if the female is allowed to brood naturally rather than attempting artificial incubation. The young, each about 70 cm (28 in) in length, hatch in about 60 days. Albino and pied specimens are becoming quite common, and some experts are entering into the realm of reptilian color breeding with this species. The Indian

Python molurus bivittatus. Photo by B. Kahl.

Python is highly recommended for beginners, providing the necessary space is available.

Python regius
ROYAL PYTHON
LENGTH: max: 2 m (6.5 ft); avg: 1.2 m (4 ft)
DESCRIPTION: Due to its small size and docility, this is a popular terrarium subject—even newly captured specimens rarely attempt to bite. It is a robust species and is a dark brown color broken by large, irregular blotches of yellowish buff to cream with darker centers.
RANGE: West Africa.
HABITAT: Found in forest, open forest, and brushland. Although it can climb well, it is primarily terrestrial, frequenting burrows and cavities in the ground where it hunts for small mammals. Mainly nocturnal, though it sometimes suns itself during the day. When captured it has a habit of

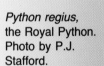

Python regius, the Royal Python. Photo by P.J. Stafford.

rolling itself into a ball with the head hidden in its coils; this gives it the alternative common name of Ball Python.

CAPTIVE CARE: Requires a medium-sized terrarium with climbing branches, a water bath, and a hollow log for hiding. Daytime temperature to 30°C (86°F), reduced to about 24°C (75°F) at night. You may try to grow robust plants with this species. It is often an "awkward" feeder in the initial stages and may steadfastly refuse all food. One method worth trying is to put the snake into a secure bag with a dead mouse; the mouse usually will be eaten in the night.

REPRODUCTION: Not bred in captivity as frequently as it ought to be. Like most pythons, it incubates its eggs by coiling around them. The young are just 30 cm (12 in) in length on hatching and should be reared on very small mice.

Python sebae

AFRICAN ROCK PYTHON
LENGTH: max: 7 m (23 ft); avg: 5 m (16.5 ft)
DESCRIPTION: Very similar in form, size, and color to

P. molurus, but the pattern is somewhat different. Captive hybrids of the two species are fairly common.

RANGE: Many suitable parts of Africa south of the Sahara.

HABITAT AND HABITS: Found in many habitats, but seems to prefer open brushland, rocky gorges, and ravines near water, which it often enters. Mainly nocturnal; it is more aggressive than *P. molurus* but will tame well if frequently handled.

Python regius.

GENERAL CARE: As described for *P. molurus*.
BREEDING: Less frequently bred in captivity than *P. molurus*. The average clutch number seems to be about 40 eggs, but as many as 100 have been reported.

Python reticulatus

RETICULATED PYTHON
LENGTH: max: 10 m (33 ft); avg: 6 m (19.5 ft)
DESCRIPTION: This is the longest of all living serpents—authenticated reports of specimens in excess of 10 m (33 ft) have been received. In spite of its length, however, it is relatively slender when compared to the Anaconda. The ground color is reddish brown to chestnut brown, with a reticulated pattern of black, yellow, and buff along the back. Along the flanks there is a double row of triangular or diamond-shaped white patches. The large, powerful head is light brown with a narrow black stripe running down the top and another running from the rear of the eye to the corner of the mouth.
RANGE: Tropical Southeast Asia, from Thailand through the Malayan Archipelago to the Philippines.
HABITAT AND HABITS: An inhabitant of the rainforest, usually close to water, which it enters freely. It sometimes enters villages, robbing poultry houses and even taking dogs, cats, and other domestic animals. There are a few proven cases of human predation. Mainly nocturnal, it is an adept climber and swimmer. Wild specimens have a vicious reputation and can give a nasty bite. Wild specimens in excess of 2 m (6.5 ft) should be handled by two or more people to prevent accidents from biting and/or constriction. In spite of this, young specimens handled frequently often will become tame and docile.
GENERAL CARE: Housing should be as described for other large python species, but with a very large, drainable water bath. Heating as described for *P. molurus*. Humidity should be high.
REPRODUCTION: Reproductive habits similar to *P. molurus*, but breeds less readily in captivity. Can lay up to 100 eggs. In

> "A newly acquired snake should be placed in a simple terrarium with minimum equipment."

captivity females seem much less inclined to incubate satisfactorily, and the eggs are often scattered and abandoned. If this happens, the eggs should be removed for artificial incubation, and a moderate hatch rate should be expected. Gravid females should be disturbed as little as possible in the hope that they will then lay and incubate normally.

Python curtus

BLOOD PYTHON

LENGTH: max: 2.8 m (9 ft); avg: 1.8 m (6 ft)

DESCRIPTION: This is a very thick python in relation to its length. It has a relatively narrow snout, but the rear part of the head is wide and flat. The tail is very short. The reddish ground color is broken by black and beige irregular bands and blotches.

RANGE: Malayan Peninsula, Sumatra, and Borneo.

HABITAT AND HABITS: A nocturnal snake that occurs at the forest margins always near or in water. This is an unpredictable species, and it can be aggressive.

Handle with care!

GENERAL CARE: Requires a medium to large, humid terrarium with a deep, preferably drainable, water bath. Although it is not an adept climber, a couple of hollow logs can be provided for hiding places and for decorative purposes. Maintain the water temperature at 25°C (77°F), air temperature up to 30°C (86°F), reduced to about 22°C (72°F) at night. Feed on mice, rats, and chickens, depending on the size of the snake. Like the Royal Python, this is a notoriously "difficult" feeder. Be sure to have adequate hiding places

Reticulated python, *Python reticulatus*. Photo by H. Hansen, Aquarium Berlin.

The Carpet Python, *Morelia spilotes f. variegata.* Photo by Dr. Sherman A. Minton.

for the snake so it can feed from undercover. REPRODUCTION: This is an oviparous brooding species like other pythons, but it seems to be bred rarely in captivity. More research into its reproductive behavior is required.

Morelia spilotes
CARPET PYTHON, DIAMOND PYTHON
LENGTH: max: 4 m (13 ft); avg: 2 m (6.5 ft)
DESCRIPTION: There are two subspecies (or color varieties—opinions differ) that are so different in coloration that they even have different common names. The Diamond Python, *M. s. spilotes*, is a glossy olive-black marked with numerous bright yellow diamond-shaped spots. The Carpet Python, *M. s. variegata*, is variegated in various shades of brown, buff, and gray. There is much variation in color and pattern, especially where the ranges of the two overlap. In spite of their length, these pythons have a relatively slender form.
RANGE: Australia, excepting the western quarter and southern Victoria; also occurs in New Guinea.
HABITAT AND HABITS: Has a very wide range of habitats from wet forest to scrubland and semi-desert. May be arboreal or terrestrial, depending on the habitat. It is mostly nocturnal or crepuscular, hiding in the burrows of other animals or in hollow limbs during the day.
GENERAL CARE: Requires a roomy terrarium with medium humidity and a large, heated water vessel (water temperature 25°C (77°F). Air temperature around 28°C (82°F), dropped to 22°C (72°F) at

night. A seasonal drop of about 5°C (9°F) in the winter for two or three months wil! be beneficial. Feed on mice, rats, and chickens, depending on the size of the snake.

REPRODUCTION: Like other pythons it is a brooder, coiling around its stack of eggs to incubate them. Gravid females should be disturbed as little as possible so their brooding instinct is not interrupted.

RELATED SPECIES: The large Australian Amethystine Python, *Liasis amethystinus*, which has reached a length of 8.5 m (27.5 ft) but averages about 3.5 m (11 ft), is not likely to become available to the average enthusiast but deserves a mention as it is one of the "giants." It comes from the tropical rainforest areas of Northern Queensland. Other, smaller Australian species include Children's Python, *Python childreni*, and the Olive Python, *Python olivaceous*. These require similar but less spacious housing to that of *M. spilotes*.

Chondropython viridis
GREEN TREE PYTHON
LENGTH: max: 2 m (6.5 ft);

The Tree Python in its blue phase, *Chondropython viridis*. Photo by P. J. Stafford.

avg: 1.2 m (4 ft)

DESCRIPTION: Bears a remarkable resemblance to the Emerald Tree Boa, *Corallus caninus*, especially when one considers that they are in different subfamilies and come from different continents. The body is laterally compressed, and the broad head is set off

HABITAT AND HABITS: A truly arboreal species that is mainly active at night, it is found only in thick rainforest regions. When at rest, it coils its body symmetrically over a branch with its head near the center of the coils.

GENERAL CARE: Requires a tall, humid terrarium with adequate climbing

Chondropython viridis, the Green Tree Python. Photo by R. Anderson.

by a narrow neck. The ground color is bright green; there is a yellow or white broken vertebral stripe.

RANGE: New Guinea, Solomon Islands, northern tip of Queensland.

branches and robust plants. Maintain daytime temperature around 28°C (82°F), reduced to 22°C (72°F) at night. Feed on mice and birds.

REPRODUCTION: Although it coils and broods the eggs like other pythons, it

is an erratic captive breeder and will soon abandon the eggs if unduly disturbed. In such cases they should be artificially incubated. The newly hatched young are brick-red in color, taking on the adult green coloration as they grow.

SUBFAMILY TROPIDOPHINAE— WOOD SNAKES OR DWARF BOAS

Although their small size would suggest otherwise, wood snakes seem to rarely be kept in captivity. Most of them are small and secretive. There are altogether about 20 species in the genera *Tropidophis, Trachyboa, Exiliboa,* and *Ungaliophis.* They are found in the Caribbean area, Central America, and northern South America. They feed mainly on lizards and small frogs, which probably accounts for their scarcity in captivity.

The Rubber Boa, *Charina bottae*, usually is delicate in captivity and requires the proper humidity levels. Photo: K. Lucas, Steinhart Aquarium.

Terrarium Construction and Maintenance

A terrarium can be described as a container in which living plants and creatures are kept in an environment as nearly like the natural habitat as possible. Snakes are notoriously non-adaptable to alien climates, so it is important that a suitable

To many snake keepers the word terrarium merely means a dry aquarium. Probably most amateur herpetologists start out by modifying a leaker aquarium into a snake cage. With proper attention to humidity and light levels and the construction of a proper lid, aquaria will serve adequately for many boids.

confined animal relies totally on its keeper for its well-being. Many species of python and boa are endangered in the wild, and every captive specimen should be treated as if it were a priceless possession. Also, all members of a family should be consulted and an agreement arrived at before specimens are acquired. Do not suddenly arrive home with a 3 m (10 ft) snake and expect all members of the family to instantly fall in love with it! Many animals have fallen by the wayside due to disputes within the family, so bear this in mind. Also, bear in mind that many boid species reach an enormous size and require correspondingly large accommodations and food items. If a snake reaches a size too large for your premises you are faced with the problem of how to dispose of it; many large specimens in zoos are abandoned "pets."

Terrarium technology has advanced a long way since the simple glass-fronted box containing a light bulb for heating and

simulated climate is provided in their housing.

Before discussing housing and the acquisition of specimens further, a word of warning. Snakes should only be kept by people who are dedicated and will remain dedicated to their welfare. Anyone who keeps captive animals of any sort has a very responsible task, bearing in mind that the

The heavily planted, almost natural, terrarium is known as a vivarium. This is not necessarily the best surroundings in which to keep a snake, although it certainly is the most attractive. Humidity levels often are very high in such planted terraria, the vegetation requires as much or more attention than the animals, and a secretive snake can literally disappear into the shrubbery for weeks at a time. Photo: B. Kahl.

Large snakes require large terraria, but large boas and pythons require less space than colubrid snakes of the same length. The inactivity of large boas and pythons is notorious.

lighting. It is now possible to purchase luxurious terraria with electronically controlled environments. Most enthusiasts still prefer to construct their own terraria, however. The advantages of this are that they can be made to a pattern exactly suited to the species being kept; they can be constructed to fit into a certain alcove or area in the home; and, above all, the expense can be kept to a minimum. Terrarium construction materials need not be expensive, and some perfectly adequate and attractive terraria have been constructed from second-hand building materials.

THE ALL—GLASS TERRARIUM

A terrarium constructed completely with glass is suitable for some of the smaller species such as sand boas and dwarf boas. An aquarium tank can be utilized, but as this is enclosed on all sides it has its limitations with regard to ventilation. With an aquarium building material called silicone rubber sealing compound, available from most pet shops, you can construct an all-glass tank of almost any shape and size. The edges of the glass are simply stuck together with the compound and held together with adhesive tape until it sets. One or two of the ends or the back of the tank can be constructed from acrylic sheeting (Plexi-Glas) into which ventilation holes can easily be drilled. The disadvantage of using Plexi-Glas for the whole structure is that with wear and regular cleaning

Tree boas from tropical forests can be housed in tall terraria with open water at the base to maintain a high humidity. Photo: B. Kahl.

it will become opaque, spoiling the view into the terrarium. The front viewing panel at least should therefore be made of glass. The shape and size of the terrarium will depend on the species being kept. A low terrarium, 100 × 60 × 50 cm (39 × 24 × 20 in) high, for example, will be suitable for a pair of sand boas, while a tall terrarium 100 × 60 × 100 cm (39 × 24 × 39 in) high would be suitable for small arboreal species and the young of larger arboreal species. Glass terraria are ideal for those species that require humid conditions.

A tight-fitting but well ventilated top to such a terrarium is essential. This should preferably

With the addition of a lighted hood or other method of heating, this basic terrarium would suffice for a small Boa Constrictor or even a sand boa. Climbing branches would make an excellent addition. Photo: J. Dommers.

apparatus is separated from the inmates by mesh. In other cases, heating and lighting apparatus can be simply suspended over the mesh lid.

THE WOODEN TERRARIUM

Glass-fronted wooden terraria are easy to construct and can be made to look most attractive. They are, however, only suitable for those species that require low to medium humidity, as the wood will otherwise be prone to rot from the dampness. Wooden terraria can be free-standing or constructed to fit into an alcove in the house. Glass access and viewing panels can be framed or unframed, sliding or hinged. During construction, one should ensure that there are no gaps left through which the snakes could escape.

The simplest free-standing wooden terrarium is virtually a box with a glass viewing panel in the front. It may be constructed from 5 mm (quarter-inch) plywood glued and tacked to a 2.5

consist of an outer wooden frame with the major part covered with mesh or screening. For very small species nylon or plastic mesh is adequate, but for larger species metal screening should be used. Perforated zinc or metal fly screening is ideal. For very large species, the use of 1 cm (0.5 in) galvanized welded mesh is recommended as some individuals may be strong enough to push a hole through weaker materials. With careful planning it is possible to build the lid in a box shape, with the heating and lighting apparatus being concealed inside. The

× 2.5 cm (1 × 1 in) framework or, preferably, 10 mm (half-inch) plywood simply glued and tacked together without a frame. Hardboard or chipboard may also be used, but as these materials are more prone to damp they must be given coatings of primer, undercoat, and a couple of topcoats of good, non-toxic gloss paint. Plywood should be can be drilled through it. For esthetic purposes it is best to measure out the positions of the holes with a ruler and mark them with a pencil so they can be drilled in symmetrical rows. Alternatively, larger squares of plywood can be cut out and the holes covered with mesh. A narrow frame of beading will tidy up the edges of the mesh where they are stapled to the plywood.

given at least two coats of clear exterior marine varnish. Whether the timber is stained to match the furniture in the room can be left entirely up to the individual.

An advantage of plywood in terrarium construction is that ventilation holes simply

THE BRICK TERRARIUM

Perhaps the most satisfying type of home terrarium, especially if one intends to keep a large species of boid, is one constructed from substantial materials such as bricks and concrete blocks. Such a

"Perhaps the most satisfying type of home terrarium...is one constructed from substantial materials such as bricks and concrete blocks."

After the hobbyist has gotten used to snakes and has outgrown his first terrarium made from a discarded aquarium, he or she often moves on to wooden terraria constructed to fit the number and type of snakes being kept. The advantage of self-built terraria is their flexibility; the disadvantage is a requirement for construction ability and time. Photo: J. Dommers.

"Hardboard or chipboard may also be used."

A beautiful specimen of a Rainbow Boa, *Epicrates cenchris*, in its dark color pattern. Photo by Jeremy Dodd.

Advanced hobbyists, especially those interested in breeding snakes, often elect to construct a snake room. An entire wall may be turned into a battery of cages and the whole room heated to the proper level. Photo: R. W. Applegate.

terrarium may be built in an alcove or be free-standing in the living area, a conservatory, or greenhouse. In warmer (frost-free) climates it may even be constructed on the patio or outside altogether, so that the inmates can benefit from natural weather conditions. The advantages of such a terrarium are that it can be constructed in any style to match any situation. With a solid concrete floor, a drainable, natural looking pond can be incorporated; natural looking rockwork, cliff faces, and controllable refuges can be included; and plant troughs can be both built in and placed

Selection of the proper substrate is important and will vary with the type of snake kept. Although moderately coarse, smooth gravel often is recommended and is readily available, many snake keepers feel that the best substrate is just a couple of sheets of newspaper. Paper is cheap and can be changed every day or as required. The snake has no concept of the substrate as long as it has a box in which to hide and a place to burrow if necessary. Photo: J. Dommers.

at decorative points outside the terrarium. There is no limit to the designs of such terraria, and some of the finest displays seen by the author have been designed and built by the owners. One design even included a tropical rainforest exhibit for Green Tree Pythons, complete with a waterfall, lush plants, and underwater viewing into the pond containing turtles. It is best to make a rough sketch plan of your terrarium before starting to build it. If you have any technical difficulties with any aspect of it, you can always consult a specialist in the appropriate building trade. In the author's experience such people are often willing to give their advice free of charge for such a fascinating project!

As an example of a built-in terrarium, let us imagine that we have an alcove somewhere in the house with dimensions of

"It is best to make a rough sketch plan of your terrarium before starting to build it."

"One or two of the ends or the back of the tank can be constructed from acrylic sheeting (Plexi-Glas) into which ventilation holes can easily be drilled."

2.5 × 1.5 m (approx. 8 × 5 ft). Assuming that the floor is solid (a brick terrarium is best suited to a solid concrete floor; do not attempt to build one on a wooden floor!), three low walls should be built to the height you require the bottom of your terrarium to be for best effect (usually about 1 m, 3 ft). The two end walls will be abutted to the existing wall, the third one in the center. Use mortar to cement the bricks together (three parts building sand to one part cement) and use a spirit level to keep the courses level. When the cement has set, lay a suitable size sheet (or sheets) of 10 mm (half-inch) plywood on top of the walls to cover the whole area. Screw a plank about 10 cm (4 in) wide along the front of the plywood to form shuttering for your concrete floor. Make a hole in the plywood base where the deepest part of the pond is going to be (for the drain) and put in a drain pipe leading to an existing drain (you may have to go through the wall of the house—if in

doubt, consult a plumber). A gate valve should be fitted to the drain pipe beneath the cage. Use as wide a pipe as possible; you should aim for a minimum diameter of 4 cm (1.5 in). The drain hole should be blocked with newspaper or cloth while you are doing the concreting to prevent blockages.

Cover the plywood with plastic sheeting (for damp-proofing) and then fill the area with concrete (four parts clean pea shingle, two parts building sand, one part cement) and level it off with a trowel. The drain pipe should just come to the surface of your concrete base, which will be about 10 cm (4 in) thick. Allow the concrete to set before constructing the pond and internal decor. This can be made from natural rocks cemented together, or you can use old bricks, etc., totally covered with a layer of concrete. If the concrete is mixed to a pliable (not too wet) consistency, you can use your artistic talents and sculpt it into almost natural-looking rock

Heavily planted terraria are set up in much the same fashion as an aquarium, with the larger plants to the back and a clear observation space in front. Many keepers recommend that plants be kept in pots and not actually planted, as they should be rotated every few weeks to reduce the bad effects of high humidity.

formations. Cement coloring can be added to the concrete (two or three different subtle shades of browns, grays, and yellows merged together

Only a few appropriate plants for the terrarium will be available at your pet shop. Some of the tougher emergent aquatic plants will do nicely for a few weeks in humid terraria.

in different areas) to make it look even more like natural rock.

The floor of the terrarium should slope down into the pond for drainage purposes. Be sure to supply smooth, level shelves or flat bottomed caves for your snakes to rest on (or in). Stout, bizarre shaped branches can be secured in the cage for climbing and further resting spots. For smaller species you will be able to provide areas for robust plants.

The front of the terrarium is given a timber frame, preferably of good quality hardwood. The hinged, glass-fronted doors are affixed to this. It is best to have ventilation panels both beneath and at the top of the terrarium. A small radiator installed beneath the cage will assist heating, especially if a heat convection panel is installed at the bottom front of the cage. Beneath the terrarium and above it, cupboard doors can be affixed so that you have easy access to drains, heaters, lighting apparatus, etc. You may even have a little extra room for storage. The ceiling of the terrarium should be adequately ventilated. It is best to have your heat lamps and fluorescent tubes installed just above a welded mesh ceiling.

There is an enormous variety of terrarium types, and it is impossible to give more than a few basic ideas here. You are advised to study the terraria of fellow enthusiasts or visit your local zoo, where you are sure to pick up all sorts of ideas and tips. A lot of your terrarium construction will be based on trial and error, and you will probably have to make many alterations before reaching the ideal situation.

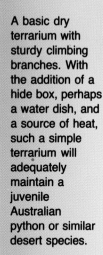

A basic dry terrarium with sturdy climbing branches. With the addition of a hide box, perhaps a water dish, and a source of heat, such a simple terrarium will adequately maintain a juvenile Australian python or similar desert species.

THE ROOM TERRARIUM

If you want to keep very large snakes and you have a spare room, you can simply use the whole room as a terrarium. First check that all possible escape routes (such as chimneys, ventilation shafts, drain holes, etc.) are blocked off. It is advisable to cover windows with mesh frames so that you can open them for ventilation without the reptiles escaping. Radiators can also be covered with a mesh guard to prevent snakes from squeezing

behind them and burning themselves. You can use a large child's wading pool as a pond, and heat lamps can be suspended over basking areas. A concrete or tiled floor is best, but a vinyl-covered wooden floor will also do, especially if it is sprinkled with a thin layer of clean sand that will facilitate cleaning. It can be swept out at regular intervals and replaced after the floor has been washed and dried.

"First check that all possible escape routes (such as chimneys, ventilation shafts, drain holes, etc.) are blocked off."

This lower terrarium without climbing branches will suffice for a sand boa or similar species. Notice that the plant is still in its pot, allowing it to be removed every few weeks for recuperation in a more favorable environment while a fresh plant is put into its place.

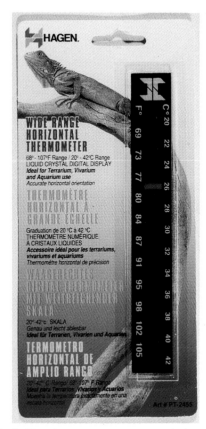

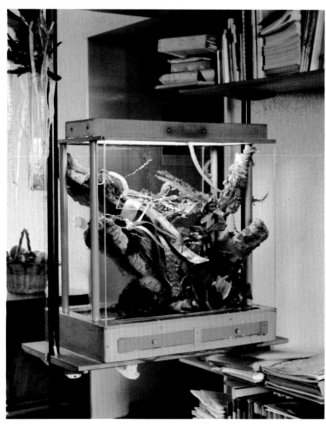

Left: Keeping an eye on your snake's ambient temperature is an important facet of good husbandry. If the animal is allowed to become too warm or too cold, it could become ill. Fortunately, high-range thermometers designed specifically for herp-keeping are now available. Photo courtesy of Hagen. Right: A correctly set up terrarium can serve as a centerpoint in the room decoration, assuming the people using the room all are used to snakes. This high planted terrarium is completely self-contained and would be suitable for a small Emerald Tree Boa, a small python, or something similar. Photo: A. van den Nieuwenhuizen.

Facing page right: Because temperature is so important to snakes, a thermometer must be in use at all times. For most simple terraria a plastic strip thermometer will suffice, but with complicated terraria where there might be significant differences in the temperatures of microhabitats (open space versus dense foliage, for instance), more delicate sensing instruments must be used.

Bottom: The typical aquarium heater can be used in some types of terraria, especially aqua-terraria and very humid terraria (where the heater can be immersed in a jar of water). In a snake terrarium it probably is best to have the thermostat and adjusting mechanism (2 and 3) at separate ends of a cable.

TERRARIUM HEATING

Unless you are lucky enough to live in the same type of climate as that of your pet's native habitat, all boid species, whether from dry or humid climates, will require some form of supplementary heating. There are as many different kinds of heating apparatus as there are terraria. The method used of course will have to be selected to suit the size of the cage. Most species will require summer daytime temperatures of 26-30°C (79-86°F), and you must have made provisions for reducing the temperature at night and during the appropriate seasons in order to simulate the natural habitat.

If you have a number of cages housing small specimens, these can simply be kept in a room that is heated to the required temperature.

Larger terraria will require a separate heating system that can be individually controlled. Such a system should be installed and tested before furnishing the terrarium and introducing the snakes. Leave the heating on for at least four hours and check temperatures with a thermometer in the cage. Only when a correct range of temperatures is arrived at should the animals be introduced. Remember that snakes can adjust to their preferred body temperature by thermoregulation, so a range of different temperatures should be provided. This can be achieved by having the heating apparatus at one end of the terrarium only, so different heat levels prevail from one end of the cage to the other. Most species require a reduction in temperature

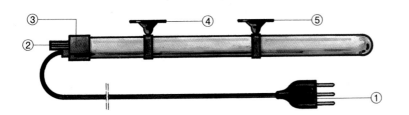

Under-tank heating pads work well with most snakes. A keeper can warm only one particular section of the enclosure, giving the inmate more than one temperature zone to chose from. Photo courtesy of Hagen.

at night; in most cases this is simply a matter of switching the heaters off at nightfall, after which the room temperature of the average household will be sufficient for the

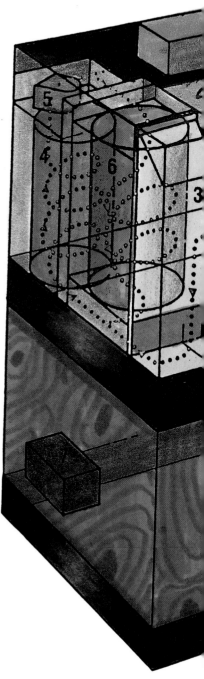

The large, complicated aquarium arrangements now available to marine aquarists can be used by herpetologists keeping sea snakes and perhaps wart snakes, but they are not suited to the keeping of even the most aquatic boids. Although the large filter system of a reef aquarium probably could handle the wastes produced by even a fairly large Anaconda, all these aquaria are lacking perhaps the most essential of snake requirements: a basking surface. Even the essentially aquatic Anaconda basks several hours a day, allowing the skin to dry and thus help prevent bacterial infections. Except for sea snakes and adult wart snakes (*Acrochordus*), all snakes need to bask or at least have the choice of basking or not.

For all practical purposes, the care of small, not very specialized boids is much like the care necessary for a garter snake or a kingsnake. Provide a terrarium large enough to move around in (meaning giving them enough room to catch their prey), provide adequate heating and lighting cycles, make sure the substrate is not dangerous and that the humidity requirements are met, and provide proper nourishment. Don't forget the hide box.

"One method of supplying warmth at night is to use a separate red or blue bulb that can be left on when other heaters are switched off."

night. If cages are kept in unheated outdoor sheds, however, where temperatures are likely to fall excessively, subdued heating at night will be necessary. For most species of python and boa, temperatures below 12°C (54°F) for a protracted period will be fatal.

The use of time switches and thermostats is highly recommended. These will enable one to ensure a regularity of day and

night temperatures that is not so easy to achieve manually. However, seasonal temperature adjustments will still be necessary for some species.

The traditional way of heating terraria was ordinary tungsten light bulbs. They do have certain advantages in that they are cheap to buy, they supply light as well as heat, and they are available in various sizes. You can produce the correct temperatures by experimenting with one or more bulbs of different wattages. Disadvantages are that they cannot be left on all night as they will destroy the photoperiod cycle, and the quality of light they emit is unsuitable for plants and for basking reptiles. However, they can be very useful for supplementary lighting and heating. One method of supplying warmth at night is to use a separate red or blue bulb (to minimize the light output) that can be left on when other heaters are switched off. Another method of utilizing the heat but not the light is to have the bulb contained inside a metal canister. Needless to say, all heat and light sources should be caged behind metal screen or mesh to minimize the possibility of the snakes burning themselves.

Infra-red lamps are also useful for terrarium heating, but these should preferably be placed outside the main body of the cage, shining through wire mesh. The types of lamps used by poultry hatcheries and pig producers are ideal. Some emit red light, others white light, but all produce radiant heat that is useful to snakes by raising or lowering the lamp. Do not direct the rays of any radiant heat apparatus onto the foliage of terrarium plants as these will quickly become desiccated. It is possible to obtain ceramic bulb heaters and similar items made especially for terraria; these are useful for maintaining nighttime warmth because they emit heat rays but no light.

An important aspect of heating in terraria requiring water and high humidity is the heating of the water itself. It is all very well to have a heated airspace, but those species that like to bathe will quickly become chilled if they enter a large body of unheated water. This will render them lethargic, unable to move adequately, and make them lose their appetite. Small bodies of water can be heated using aquarium heaters and

Floor room is the important part of the terrarium for a terrestrial snake, not the volume of the container.

Hide boxes are essential and can be of any material or construction as long as they have a hole of the proper size for the snake to enter when it needs privacy.

Take out the water and the submersed plants, and this aquarium would be adequate for some boids.

"An important aspect of heating in terraria requiring water and high humidity is the heating of the water itself."

A terrarium is not an aquarium, although there are similarities. You will almost never have a snake that requires being kept mostly in water. Even the most aquatic species require access to basking areas to dry the skin. The normal steps in aquarium preparation, such as washing the gravel and sweeping it carefully into the corners, are unnecessary with snakes that will immediately dirty the gravel and rearrange it anyway. An aquarium heater cannot be safely operated in the air, so if used in the terrarium it must be put in a jar of water or a basin.

"For most tropical snakes, the water temperature should not drop below 22°C (72°F) day or night."

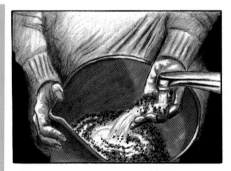

thermostats. The addition of an aquarium aerator to the pond will raise air humidity and temperature and provide a certain amount of ventilation. Glass aquarium heaters (and thermostats) should be protected from breakage by placing them inside a plastic or earthenware pipe in the water.

If you keep very large semi-aquatic boids (Anacondas, Reticulated Pythons, etc.) that require a large volume of water, you will have to provide a more substantial means of maintaining water temperature. A circulating waterfall with the return pipes passing through a thermostatically controlled immersion heater tank is the best method to use. For most tropical snakes, the water temperature should not drop below 22°C (72°F) day or night.

TERRARIUM LIGHTING

Although most species of boid are crepuscular or nocturnal, good light cycles are important to all species whether nocturnal or diurnal. Although natural sunlight can be beneficial to your snakes, remember that it can be lethal in the small confines of the terrarium left in full sunlight for too long. It is best to provide a compromise system of lighting using a combination of tungsten bulbs and fluorescent tubes. Broad-spectrum fluorescent tubes (daylight quality) of the type used by horticulturists are ideal as they emit a certain amount of ultraviolet rays sufficient in quantity and quality to keep your reptiles' skins in good health. They also enhance the color and pattern of the snakes for the

HUMIDITY

Species from tropical rainforest areas require a high air humidity. At the same time, they must have dry areas of substrate on which they can rest, otherwise they may be prone to skin infections. If a large heated pool is available, the provision of

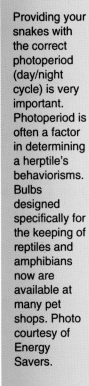

Providing your snakes with the correct photoperiod (day/night cycle) is very important. Photoperiod is often a factor in determining a herptile's behaviorisms. Bulbs designed specifically for the keeping of reptiles and amphibians now are available at many pet shops. Photo courtesy of Energy Savers.

observer. Such lamps are essential if you intend to grow living plants in the terrarium.

Mercury vapor and quartz-halogen lamps may be considered for use in large terraria. These emit a greater intensity of light than most other lamps. They may have wattages of 500 or more, may emit a high temperature, and are expensive to run. Such lamps will promote lush growth of terrarium plants providing the distance from them is great enough to prevent burning of the foliage.

extra humidifiers is unnecessary as the air will be kept humid by the slow evaporation of the water. For small arboreal boids, an **aquarium** heater set in the water vessel will provide adequate humidity, especially if used in conjunction with an aerator.

VENTILATION

Whether a terrarium is meant to be dry or humid, adequate ventilation is necessary so that the air does not become stale and possibly laden with infectious organisms. A

Organic substrates like crushed bark are ideal for snakes. Most organic substrates are easy to work with, pleasing to the eye, and can be bought in bulk quantities. Photo courtesy of Four Paws.

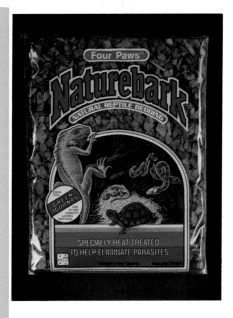

Setting up a dry terrarium is relatively simple. First make sure the tank is clean and has no chemical residues of any type. Your substrate goes down first, followed by the rocks, etc. If you plan on piling up rocks, use silicone cement to fix them into position and avoid accidentally crushed snakes.

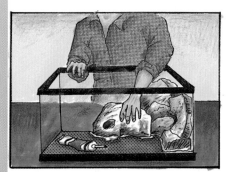

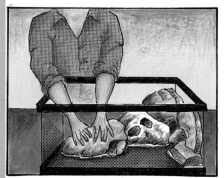

terrarium can be ventilated simply by having adequate air vents at appropriate positions in the walls, but cold drafts coming directly into the terrarium must be avoided. Try and keep your terrarium in an area that is not subject to excessive household or tobacco fumes.

TERRARIUM FURNISHINGS

Many species of boids have been successfully bred in a terrarium with the barest essentials. Apart from the necessary life-support systems, a paper floor covering, a climbing branch, a hide-box, and a water dish are all that are essential. Indeed, if you keep a breeding colony, this is really the only sensible way of keeping them. However, most terrarium keepers like to have at least one decorative terrarium in which they can make an attractive compromise facsimile of the snake's native habitat.

Substrate Materials

For small desert-living species such as sand boas, clean, coarse, dry sand to a depth of about 15 cm (6 in) can be used. It must, however, be replaced at regular intervals as it will soon become fouled from the snake's droppings. For larger boids and for humid terraria, it is recommended that washed gravel be used (gravel is better as it is smoother and less abrasive on the snakes' skins than crushed stone). Gravel can be obtained in various grades; 5 mm (quarter-inch) pea gravel, suitable for small species, up to 25 mm (1 inch) grade for large snakes. One advantage of gravel over peat, earth, and sand is that the snake does not drag it about the terrarium when it leaves the water. Always keep a spare stock of clean gravel so you can replace it at monthly intervals. The soiled gravel can be washed under running water and dried out, ready for use again.

Tree Branches

These can be used for decorative purposes, as supports for climbing terrarium plants, and as climbing facilities for arboreal species. The size and strength of the branches must, of course, reflect the size and weight of the snake. Try and find bizarrely shaped branches with horizontal limbs on which the snakes can rest. The sea shore and river beds are good places to look for branches that have been naturally polished and

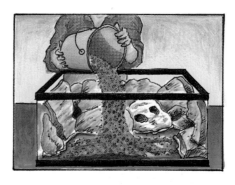

bleached. All branches should be thoroughly scrubbed and dried out before being used in the terrarium. Hollow logs are useful as hiding places, but ensure that such hiding places are accessible to you should you need to remove the snake at any time. Branches should be secured in the terrarium

"For larger boids and for humid terraria, it is recommended that washed gravel be used."

If you are planning on constructing an aqua-terrarium, it might be best to cement the rocks directly to the bottom of the tank and then add the substrate last.

"Hollow logs are useful for hiding places, but ensure that such hiding places are accessible to you should you need to remove the snake at any time."

"Natural rocks can be used to good effect in the terrarium for decorative purposes, as raised basking sites, and, cemented together to form caves, as controllable hiding places."

"Be sure to have controllable hiding places so you always have access to the snakes."

If you keep a boa or python that even occasionally climbs, you should provide it with a sturdy climbing branch. Remember that even a small python such as this *Python regius*, the Ball Python, can weigh several pounds and its activity can disturb or even break a weak branch.

as stably as possible so that they do not fall down when the reptiles climb on them.

Rocks

Natural rocks can be used to good effect in the terrarium for decorative purposes, as raised basking sites, and, cemented together to form caves, as controllable hiding places. Rocks can be purchased from pet shops and from garden centers, or they can be collected from the countryside.

of a single type rather than mix them. Rocks should be arranged in such a way that they cannot fall down and injure the reptiles. Large conglomerations of rocks are best cemented together. This makes them safer and eliminates many cracks and crannies where dirt can accumulate and parasites can lurk. With the judicious use of cement coloring, you should be able to reproduce the color of the rocks so that they look like a solid

They come in all shapes, sizes, and types but, for the best esthetic affect, it is advisable to use rocks

mass. Be sure to have controllable hiding places so you always have access to the snakes.

Basking sites are essential. Except for sea snakes and wart snakes, all snakes (probably including most burrowers) bask at least occasionally. Even aquatic snakes will bask on top of aquatic plants. Photo: E. C. Taylor.

Plants

Plants add a subtle finishing touch to the terrarium, but sometimes they are more difficult to keep alive than the snakes themselves. In any case, it is futile to try and grow plants in a terrarium containing the larger boids; they will soon be crushed and killed by the movement of the snakes. In such cases you can make the terrarium look more attractive by using strong, natural-looking plastic plants inside and having natural plants in pots arranged outside the terrarium to break up the straight outlines.

For small arboreal boids, robust house plants of many species may be used. Try and choose those that are suited to the same climate and conditions as the snakes. You can plant cacti and/or succulents in a cage containing sand boas. Plants in the terrarium should be kept in pots to minimize disturbance from the snakes and to allow them to be easily removed when necessary. When constructing rockwork with cement, cavities can be made to fit the plant pots exactly. It is advisable to keep spare plants so that they can do "shifts" of say two weeks at a time, allowing them to recover from the rigors of life in a snake terrarium before being used again. A book on house plant care will give you many tips on maintaining plants indoors.

Feeding live foods is not a simple process. First, there is the possibility that the prey will turn into the predator. Mammals, including mice and especially rats, are more intelligent and adaptable than any snake. If they manage to hide long enough for the snake to lose interest or cool down at night, they can attack and cause serious damage or occasionally even death through their bites. Second, many people and organized groups actively oppose feeding of living mammals and birds to snakes on personal ethical grounds. These persons and groups have caused laws to be passed in some areas that restrict and even penalize overt feeding of mammals and birds to snakes.

General Care and Feeding

SELECTION AND ACQUISITION OF SPECIMENS

There are about 90 different species of pythons and boas; some of these are quite common in the wild, easy to keep in captivity, and relatively easy to breed. Others are scarce in the wild; some are even in danger of

Unusual species of boids sometimes are available from specialist dealers. The Australian Carpet Python, *Morelia spilotes,* is seldom exported legally, but occasionally captive-bred specimens become available to advanced hobbyists. The beginner should try only the most common species first until he learns the basics of boid husbandry. Photo: R. T. Hoser.

extinction, and, ironically, it is just these species that seem to be more difficult to maintain in the terrarium. It is therefore highly recommended that the beginner to boid keeping concentrate on the common species before attempting his luck with the rarer species.

Many countries have their specialist dealers in reptiles and amphibians, and some pet shops may have just a few specimens. It will certainly be worth just spending a few days shopping around before deciding what to buy. Avoid dealing with shops that are dirty, untidy, and have large numbers of smelly, unhealthy looking specimens in inadequate cages. Unfortunately there are still a few such places about, but the majority of modern dealers have clean, hygienic premises and really care for their stock, presenting it in clean, attractive terraria. Such dealers are always pleased to answer specific questions about their various stock.

A snake should be examined very carefully before it is purchased so that we can be sure of taking a healthy specimen home. Look for signs of mites or ticks on the reptiles or in the cage. Choose only those with clean, unbroken skin. Ensure that the reptile is alert, clear-eyed, and plump, and avoid specimens that show no interest in your attention. Tongue flickering, fight, and flight are all signs that a reptile is alert and healthy. Ask if the snake is feeding (most dealers will answer yes to this question whether it is or not, but there is no harm in asking) and examine the mouth for signs of inflammation that could indicate mouth rot. If possible, have a trial handling session in the shop; the dealer will probably show you what to do and it will give you an idea of whether you are competent in restraining the snake.

"Ensure that the reptile is alert, clear-eyed, and plump, and avoid specimens that show no interest in your attention."

This Diamond Python, *Morelia spilotes,* clearly shows the vertical or slit pupil typical of most boas and pythons. Such a pupil is characteristic of snakes that hunt at night or under low light conditions. Photo: P. J. Stafford.

Ticks are not uncommonly found on freshly imported boas and pythons. Because they can carry diseases and cause local tissue damage, they should be removed as soon as they are discovered. Although there is a risk of infection, many hobbyists just pull out the tick and put a dab of antibiotic on the wound. Photo: W. B. Allen, Jr.

"Collecting from the wild is no longer as easy as it used to be, as most countries now have strict conservation and movement controls on most of their native fauna."

Apart from pet shops and reptile dealers, there are two other ways of obtaining stock. The best of all methods is to obtain captive-bred specimens directly from the breeder. The best way to find out who is breeding what is to join a herpetological society and discuss your requirements with other members. Even if you are too far away to attend regular meetings, most societies publish a newsletter in which breeders advertise their surplus stock. A major advantage of home-bred stock is that it is relatively easy to settle into a new terrarium, it is less likely to be infected with diseases and/or parasites, and you will be happy to know that another specimen has not been taken from the wild.

The final method of obtaining stock is the most difficult one and must be considered with great caution. Collecting from the wild is no longer as easy as it used to be, as most countries now have strict conservation and movement controls on most of their native fauna. In many countries all species are protected; in

Handling small snakes is not difficult. Obtain a firm grasp at the angles of the jaws so the head can be rigidly controlled. Depending on the size of the snake, the rest of the body can be controlled with the same hand or the body can be held with the other hand. Snakes should never be allowed to just dangle, as many species have delicate neck vertebrae that could be damaged by the snake's own weight. Snakes with prehensile tails present a problem as their tail acts like a hand and will grasp the handler. Photo by S. Kochetov.

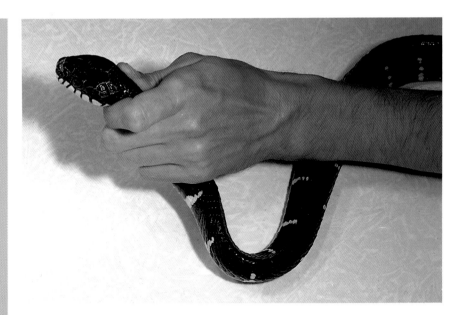

When handling dangerous species such as this Mangrove Snake, *Boiga dendrophila,* it is important to always keep complete control of the head yet not exert enough force to damage the delicate jaw bones of the snake. Knowing the right amount of force is a matter of experience that can only come through handling a variety of snakes of different species and sizes. The beginner should never handle venomous snakes or those capable of inflicting severe bites, such as Emerald Tree Boas. Photo: S. Kochetov.

"Only collect what you require for your own immediate requirements."

others, only licensed dealers are allowed to collect. Where only certain species are protected it may be possible to collect others, but before collecting make sure that you are not contravening any country or state laws or by-laws. Only collect what you require for your own immediate requirements. In some places you may collect for yourself, but it may be against the law to offer the collected specimens for sale. One advantage of collecting from the wild is that you are able to study the exact habitat and will be able to set up the terrarium accordingly.

TRANSPORT OF SPECIMENS

All too often animals are lost in transit due to thoughtless or callous packing. The most satisfactory method of transporting snakes is individually in cloth (preferably cotton) bags. Rice sacks and strong pillow cases are ideal. A number of bags, separated by partitions, can be placed in a stout cardboard carton or a wooden box. Should the package have to travel in a cold climate, it is advisable to line the box with an insulating material such as styrofoam. Be sure to select the quickest and most direct route of despatch.

If purchasing new stock, it is best to pick it up yourself if this is convenient, then you can be sure to transport it home as quickly and comfortably as possible. If shipped by freight, each bag should be individually labelled with the contents and the outer container should be clearly marked with name, address, and telephone numbers of both the consignor and consignee. Another mention that livestock should be kept warm is also advisable.

QUARANTINE

Any new stock being added to an existing collection should be quarantined before it is allowed to come into contact with healthy stock. This is to ensure

Belligerent snakes often can be handled safely by first dropping a bag or pillow case over them. Snakes often calm down in the dark and can then be carefully picked up near the head until the correct controlling position is attained. Photo: S. Kochetov.

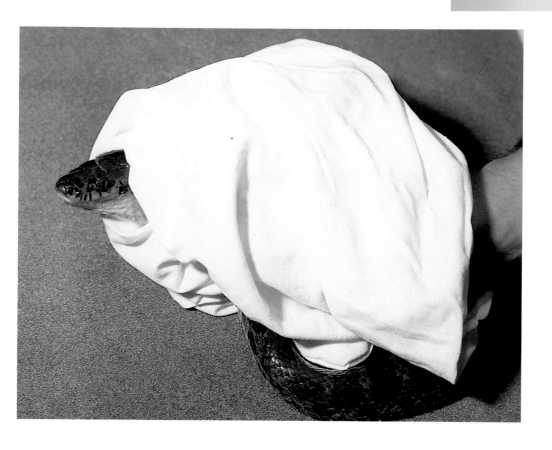

A snake stick of some type is essential for safe handling of large or aggressive snakes. Many types of snake sticks are made, but most of them consist of some form of L-shaped steel rod or angle-iron. They may be purchased or made from scrap. Photo: S. Kochetov.

that a new specimen does not introduce diseases or parasites. A newly acquired snake should be placed in a simple terrarium with minimum equipment (just enough to ensure its well-being) and kept under observation for about three weeks. If no disease symptoms appear, and if the reptile is feeding and behaving normally after this time, it may then be introduced to existing stock. Quarantine cages are best kept in a separate room to further

minimize the risk of parasitic infections.

HANDLING

New acquisitions should be given a further thorough examination on arrival at home. If any signs of parasites or disease are spotted, appropriate treatment is required. Reptiles should be inspected thereafter as often as possible to ensure that all is well. If a disease should occur, chances of a complete cure are more likely if

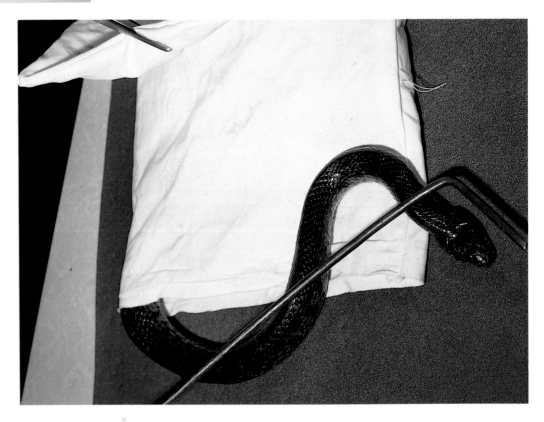

treatment starts in the early stages.

It will be necessary to handle your snakes regularly in order to tame them, to keep them tame, and to examine them at the same time. Small boids and hatchlings up to about 60 cm (24 in) in length can be picked up with one hand. If they are vicious (snakes of this size may bite but their teeth are too small to do much damage other than a few "pinpricks," but such a bite still should be wiped with an antiseptic solution for safety's sake), they should be restrained just behind the head with the thumb and forefinger; the body can then be draped over the hand.

Snakes up to 150 cm (5 ft) in length require both hands for handling. If tame they can be simply picked up roughly one-third and two-thirds along the body and draped over

Perhaps the hardest and most dangerous moment when handling a snake is when removing it from a snake bag. Caution is always advisable, as the teeth of a large snake can penetrate cotton and other loosely woven fabrics with ease. Photo: S. Kochetov.

No, the top snake is not being beaten with a board. Since control of the head is essential in handling any aggressive snake, you may be forced to use whatever is handy to pin down the head. The problems with a makeshift tool such as a board are that it is hard to handle and may accidentally damage the specimen. A snake stick, shown in use below, is much easier to control and less likely to cause serious injuries. Photos by S. Kochetov.

the arms with minimum restraint as they crawl about. Aggressive snakes of this size should be secured by the neck (just behind the head) with the whole hand; use the other hand to support the body.

Very large boids in excess of 150 cm (5 ft) are capable of giving deep, painful bites with their relatively thick, long, recurved teeth, and their powers of constriction must be treated with respect. Aggressive specimens should be handled by two people, one restraining the head to prevent biting, the other holding the body and preventing constriction. If a snake should manage to get a powerful grip with its coils on some portion of the handler's anatomy, the other handler can quickly unwind it.

In spite of the aforementioned warnings, however, most boids become remarkably docile and tame after a few handling sessions. Hatchlings that are frequently handled from birth onward are the tamest, and if the handling goes on they will remain docile even when they have reached a substantial length. Tame pythons and boas of all sizes can be simply picked up and draped about one's shoulders.

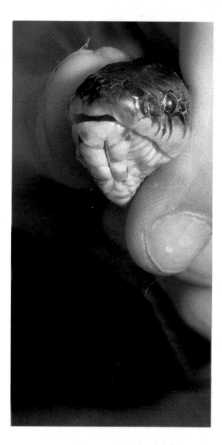

From the way the jaws of this snake are twisted, it seems that too much pressure is being applied. The jaw bones of a snake are slender and are connected to the skull and each other by long and rather delicate ligaments. Exercise care whenever handling a snake. Photo: S. Kochetov

FOODS AND FEEDING

To remain healthy, all animals require a balanced diet containing proteins, carbohydrates, fats, vitamins, and minerals. Fortunately, it is relatively easy to give

"Most boids become remarkably docile and tame after a few handling sessions."

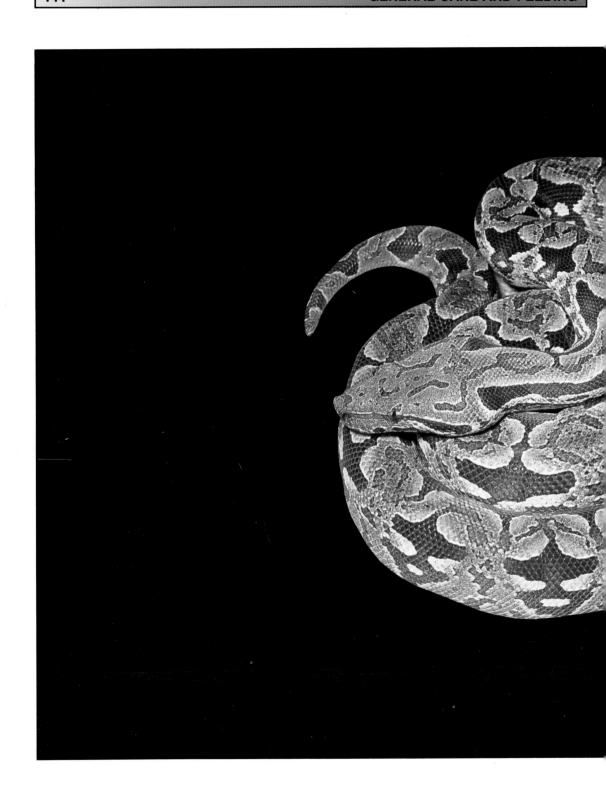

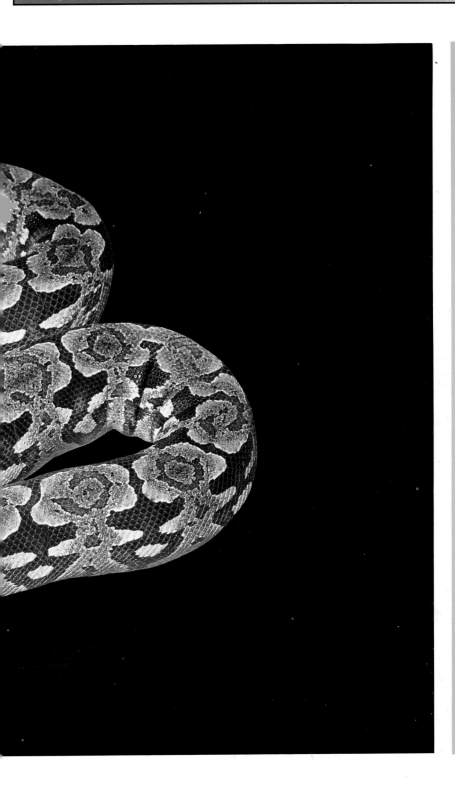

Dumeril's Boa from Madagascar. Photo by Ken Lucas at the Steinhart Aquarium.

most pythons and boas a balanced diet as they feed on whole prey animals. If the prey animals themselves have been reared on a balanced diet, then they will constitute a balanced diet in themselves.

A certain amount of controversy exists over whether live prey animals should be fed to captive snakes. The snake keeper will argue that snakes catch and kill live prey in the wild, so what difference does it make if they are allowed to do it in captivity? Another argument for it is that if you do not allow the snake to kill the prey, you may have to do it yourself and the question arises as to who would make the better job of it. The "anti-feeding-live-food-to-snakes lobby" maintains that if it is necessary to keep captive snakes alive by giving them live food, then they should not be kept at all. Fortunately, most captive boids will take dead prey and those that at first will not can usually be trained to do so. The prey is simply moved about in front of the snake's nose with a

At one time zoos fed their snakes living prey before large crowds of curious onlookers. Today such an activity would be likely to draw complaints and possibly even legal action in some areas. Snakes must eat to live, and most snakes prefer mice, rats, and chickens in captivity. Fortunately, many snakes, especially captive-bred specimens, adjust well to frozen and thawed foods, but the keeper may have to try inventive ways to make them take the strange food the first few times.

Not just rats and mice can be dangerous to snakes. Large invertebrates sometimes found in tropical plants can rarely be a source of danger. This giant centipede is large enough to kill a small or hatchling snake. The odds of accidentally introducing such a predator into the terrarium are of course small, but accidents do happen. Check all new plants and natural substrates carefully when first purchased or if left outdoors in storage. Photo: W. B. Allen, Jr.

"In some countries specialized dealers can supply quantities of deep-frozen mice or rats."

stick until a feeding response arises. Sometimes this will take an initial reaction of anger; the snake will bite the prey, realize it has something edible and proceed to swallow it.

Food for pythons and boas is relatively easy to obtain. Most species can be fed on mice, rats, chickens, or a combination of these easy to obtain animals. Laboratory mice and rats are the staple diet of many captive boids. Wild rodents are best not used as they may transmit diseases or parasites or be contaminated with insecticides or rodenticides. It is up to the individual whether he is prepared to breed sufficient quantities of rodents for the reptiles or whether they should be purchased as required. Some medical laboratories are willing to sell off excess stock cheaply. In some countries specialized dealers can supply quantities of deep-frozen mice or rats. These, of course, must be thoroughly thawed out and brought up to terrarium temperature before being fed to the snakes.

Day-old chicks can often be obtained cheaply from hatcheries either alive or to snakes than hatchlings. For large boids, chicks can be grown to a size suitable to the size of the snake. Egg farms are often a good source of "obsolete" laying hens. Fully grown specimens of the giant boids will take

The first step in force-feeding is carefully opening the mouth, making sure not to damage any teeth, which could lead to infection. Photo: S. Kochetov.

dead, and some companies deal in quantities of frozen chicks. Chicks that have been well-fed and allowed to grow for a few days are more nutritious fully grown chickens, ducks, geese, and rabbits.

Any animals kept for the purpose of feeding to snakes should be kept in clean, hygienic conditions and be given a balanced

"Chicks that have been well-fed and allowed to grow for a few days are more nutritious to snakes than hatchlings."

Step two in force-feeding is to carefully move the flat instrument (spatula, special metal instrument, spoon handle, etc.) to the back of the mouth. Photo: S. Kochetov.

diet. The fact that they are "snake food" is no excuse to neglect any animals. In any case, animals that have been kept in good condition will be more nutritious to the snakes.

but it is easy for them to become greedy and eat more than is good for them. It is more healthy for a snake to grow slowly; fast growers will become obese, sometimes to the stage where they are

"It is more healthy for a snake to grow slowly; fast growers will become obese."

FEEDING TECHNIQUES

It is difficult to provide hard and fast rules about how often snakes should be fed. Young rapidly growing snakes will feed more often than adults,

killed by excessive fat deposits in the internal organs. Obese specimens also do not make the best breeders. Most of the larger boid species can take half-grown to fully grown mice soon after hatching (snakes usually wait until after the first molt before taking the first meal). As a general guide, feed a youngster one mouse twice a week for the first few months.

well on a large goose or rabbit once every two weeks.

If food is refused after an hour or so of its being offered, it should be removed from the cage. Some boids are

Force-feeding step three: Slowly twist the instrument vertically to force the snake to open the mouth. Be very careful to do no damage. Photo: S. Kochetov.

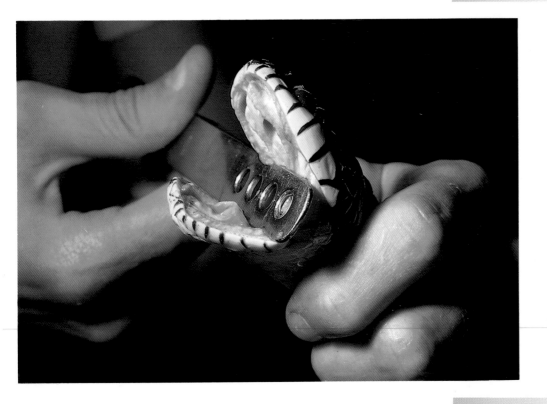

As soon as the snake reaches a suitable size it can graduate to one rat or large chick per week and, finally, to one chicken per week. Very large specimens will do quite

unpredictable and will sometimes fast for a time for no apparent reason. A large Anaconda in the author's care once voluntarily fasted for 14 months before once more

"A large Anaconda in the author's care once voluntarily fasted for 14 months."

becoming ravenous on a diet of muscovy ducks. If live food must be given, do not leave it in the cage unobserved; it is not unknown for hungry mice and rats to gnaw into the

one or two alternatives, dead or alive, daytime or nighttime, you may have to resort to force-feeding. However, before doing this, make certain that the reptile is not suffering

If no instrument is available, the mouth of larger snakes sometimes can be opened by slowly pulling on the loose tissue beneath the lower jaw. This is dangerous in species that have very delicate scalation as breaks in the scales could lead to later problems. Photo: S. Kochetov.

"Mouth rot, internal or external parasites, sloughing difficulties, etc., may all affect appetite."

body of a snake.

Occasionally, a snake will refuse all food offered. Having ascertained that you are giving it the correct food and after perhaps trying

from any obvious disease or condition that is contributing to its loss of appetite. Mouth rot, internal or external parasites, sloughing difficulties, etc., may all affect appetite, in which case treatment should precede or accompany force-feeding.

There are two basic methods of force-feeding. The first is to take a lucky, the snake will soon start swallowing under its own accord, but if not, the prey can be gradually pushed into the throat and massaged down into the gullet. Something firm

The correct way to hold a medium-sized non-aggressive snake. Note that all four "sides" of the head are under complete control. Photo: S. Kochetov.

whole, dead prey animal of suitable size and, opening the snake's mouth by pulling at the loose skin below the jaw, introduce it head-first into the mouth. If you are but not too hard, like a wooden spoon handle, can be used to push the prey gently and firmly into the snake's gullet.

The second method of force-feeding is to liquefy

Eryx conicus, juvenile, the Rough-scaled Sand Boa. Photo by P. J.Stafford.

This cleared and stained snake shows the long string of vertebrae that form most of the snake's skeleton. Note also (in bright blue) the heavy rings of cartilage that outline the esophagus, running from the floor of the mouth to the junction with the intestines. Photo: Dr. G. Dingerkus.

the prey animal and give it to the snake via a large syringe and a stomach tube. The tube which should have smooth edges and should be lubricated with mineral oil, is pushed down into the snake's stomach (about one-third along its total length) and the pulped prey is pumped into it via the syringe. The author has found a large cake-icer to be ideal for this purpose. The first time you try to use either method of force-feeding, it perhaps would be best to obtain help from a veterinarian or a more experienced herpetologist.

HYGIENE

Good hygiene is important with regard to any animals being kept in captivity, as organisms living in close proximity can easily pass a disease from one to the next. If the snakes are kept on absorbent paper this may easily be changed each time it becomes soiled. If kept on other kinds of substrate materials, fecal

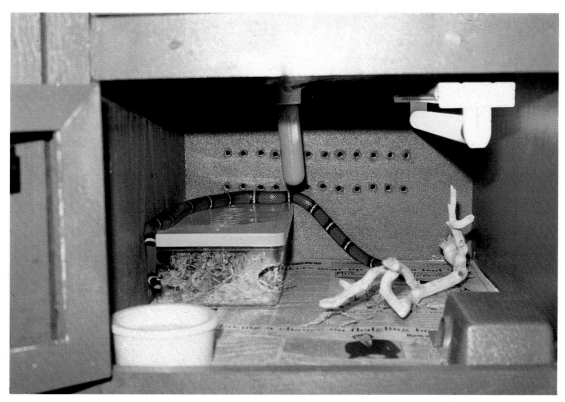

An efficient and attractive, non-natural, snake cage providing all the snake's needs. Note the lighting unit, the ceramic heater, water bowl, climbing branches, hide boxes, and paper substrate. Photo: J. Gee.

matter can be scooped out using a small shovel. Each time the cage is heavily soiled, or otherwise about once per two weeks, all materials should be removed from the cage and either discarded to be replaced or thoroughly scrubbed and disinfected. The inside of the cage should be scrubbed with warm water, detergent, and a small amount of household bleach (about 5%). Domestic disinfectants other than bleach should not be used as these could have a detrimental effect on the health of our snakes. Povidone-iodine solution can, however, be used according to the manufacturer's instructions. Whatever disinfecting material is used, it should be thoroughly rinsed away with clear water and dried before snakes are reintroduced to the cage.

"Each time the cage is heavily soiled, or otherwise about once per two weeks, all materials should be removed from the cage and either discarded to be replaced or thoroughly scrubbed and disinfected."

*Boiga
dendrophila.*
Photo by
Burkhard Kahl.

Drinking and bathing water should always be fresh and scrupulously clean. Boids seem to delight in defecating in the water vessel, so it is important to change the water regularly, preferably daily. The glass viewing panels of the terrarium should be kept crystal-clear. You will find a rubber squeegee useful for doing this.

DISEASES AND TREATMENT

Providing your snakes are kept in optimum climatic conditions, receive an adequate diet,

and strict hygienic measures are taken, they should live a long and healthy life. However, there are always cases where reptiles become sick through unforeseen circumstances. If you are unsure what to do you should consult a veterinarian. Most veterinarians do not specialize in reptile diseases, but there are some who do, and your vet will almost certainly be able to contact a specialist if he cannot do the job himself. Diseases of snakes are many and varied, but most of them are not infectious to

These tapeworm proglottids (reproductive segments) come from the feces of an Anaconda. It is common for boids to carry heavy intestinal parasite loads that do little harm until the snake is stressed. Your veterinarian can do fecal examinations for worm eggs and will recommend an effective anthelminthic drug. Photo: W. B. Allen, Jr.

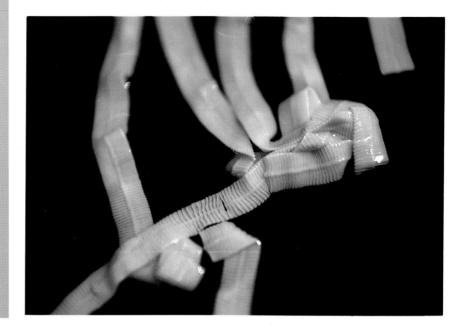

Since the transparent brille or spectacle that covers the eye is just a modified scale, it is subject both to injury and to abnormalities that occur at or before birth. In the illustrated snakes the brille has not developed as a transparent scale but is at least partially opaque (center and bottom) or indistinguishable from an ordinary opaque scale (python at top). Individuals with such abnormalities are blind. Photos by Dr. F. L. Frye from his book *Reptile Care*.

human beings. However, it is wise to wash your hands thoroughly after each handling or cleaning session, just to be on the safe side. The following are a few of the more usual ailments likely to affect your snake.

INJURIES AND WOUNDS: These may be caused by fighting

Your veterinarian will be able to diagnose the proper medications and procedures to take care of most of your snake's ills. Photo: S. Kochetov.

(especially among male boids), by live prey, and by getting jammed in some sharp corner (make sure that there are no sharp edges in the terrarium). They should be bathed in a good antiseptic solution such as povidone-iodine. Deep wounds may have to be sutured. Consult your veterinarian.

ABSCESSES AND CYSTS: These appear as hard or soft lumps under the snake's skin and have various causes. In most cases a veterinarian will recommend surgical removal. The wound is then swabbed out with antiseptic and sutured. Sometimes antibiotic treatment will also be necessary.

MOUTH ROT: Mouth rot (more properly necrotic stomatitis) usually begins when nervous snakes strike repeatedly at the terrarium glass, causing

This Puff Adder (*Bitis arietans*) has bruised tissue around the fangs that obviously is infected. This probably is the start of a bad case of mouth rot that could progress if not treated as soon as discovered. Photo: W. B. Allen, Jr.

wounds around the snout and lips that become infected. Teasing your newly acquired snake through the cage glass is an almost sure way of inflicting this sometimes fatal disease on it. Early cases, when small red spots and small areas of grayish matter are seen just inside the lips, can be treated by swabbing with a mild antiseptic such as povidone-iodine. More advanced cases will require treatment under anesthetic. Consult your veterinarian.

EXTERNAL PARASITES: Mite infestations are unfortunately common in captive boids, and in severe infestations the snakes can become stressed and anemic. The mites live in cracks and crannies in the cages and come out at night to suck blood. Each mite is globular and less than 1 mm (one-twenty-fifth of an inch) in diameter. Presence of the mites can be detected during the day by their droppings, which look like silvery dust on the surface of the scales. A badly infected snake will lose its appetite and could starve to death unless treated. Another danger from mites (and ticks) is that they can transmit blood-borne diseases from one

"Early cases (of mouth rot), when small red spots and small areas of grayish matter are seen just inside the lips, can be treated by swabbing with a mild antiseptic such as povidone-iodine."

reptile to the next. An infested snake should be moved to a clean terrarium in which a small piece of insecticide-impregnated plastic strip is suspended in such a way that the reptiles cannot come into contact with it. The miticidal gas released by the strip will kill all the mites within four days. The infested terrarium and the room in which it is kept should be thoroughly scrubbed and sprayed with miticide before being scrubbed and rinsed again.

Ticks are often found on freshly captured snakes. These attach themselves to the snakes, usually between scales (especially around the vent). Being much larger than mites, they are

"The infested terrarium and the room in which it is kept should be thoroughly scrubbed and sprayed with miticide before being scrubbed and rinsed again."

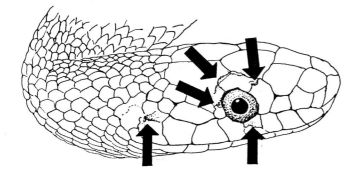

It is not uncommon to find snakes with minor irregularities of the head scalation. This can have many different causes. This snake has several fused and irregular scales around the eye and among the temporal scales. This could result from mite infestations but is more likely to be the result of an injury. Shedding problems also can cause irregular scales. Some scale defects are genetic and are passed on from parent to offspring in normal Mendelian fashion. To the keeper, such defects if minor are just a way of identifying an individual snake, much like a mole or minor scar serves as a distinguishing character for a person. Photo: B. Kahl.

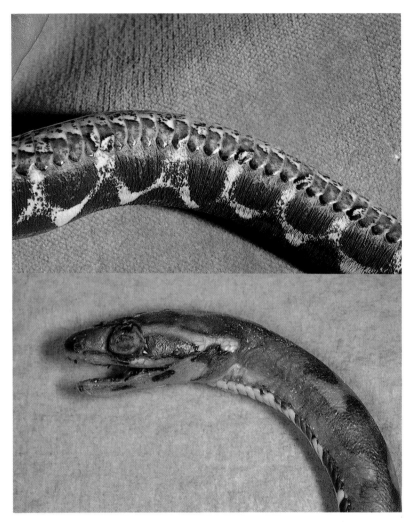

Scales are essential to the life of the snake. They serve as a barrier to infection, help in movement, often have distinctive behavioral uses, and basically make a snake a snake. However, occasionally a snake is found that either has no scales over some or all the body or has the scales reversed (pointing forward, not back). Such specimens almost always are hatchlings, as these odd specimens do not live long in nature. The pictured snakes are lacking most or all the body and head scales, although the ventral scales appear to be almost normal. Note that the color pattern is in the skin itself, not just the scales. Photos: Dr. F. L. Frye from his book *Reptile Care.*

easier to detect, and as they usually are found only in small numbers they are easier to remove. A tick can be dabbed with rubbing alcohol to make it relax its mouthparts and can then easily be removed with forceps and destroyed.

INTERNAL PARASITES: Various types of parasitic worms (helminths) commonly infect snakes. Roundworms, tapeworms, and threadworms may live in a snake's digestive system for its whole life without causing any major disability. In times of stress, however, as is likely when a snake is newly captured, the mechanism that keeps the worms at controllable levels may break down, causing the worms to grow or multiply out of proportion. Regular examination of fecal samples of snakes in a veterinary laboratory will indicate presence of worm eggs. There are a number of anthelminthic drugs available that are suitable for removing worm infestations in snakes. Consult your veterinarian about the best course to take.

The Gopher Snake (*Pituophis catenifer*) at the top lacks scales and is still living. Such animals almost always die soon after hatching in nature but if found early can be cared for in the laboratory for weeks or months. The *Elaphe* (Chicken Snake) at the bottom not only lacks most scales but also has adhesion of the lower abdomen, probably both internally and externally. Photos: Dr. F. L. Frye from his book *Reptile Care*.

A female Ball Python, *Python regius*, and one of its newly hatched offspring. Most boa and python young are very similar to the parents, with a few exceptions. The Emerald Tree Boa and Green Tree Python, for instance, begin life with bright orange to yellow coloration, gradually turning bright green over a period of a year or more. Photo: S. C. and H. Miller.

Captive Reproduction

The breeding of captive specimens is one of the most exciting and satisfying aspects of keeping boids. However, it is only reptiles that are kept in the best of health and given the necessary stimuli that will make any attempt to court and mate. A knowledge of the environmental conditions in the wild

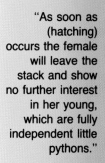

"As soon as (hatching) occurs the female will leave the stack and show no further interest in her young, which are fully independent little pythons."

Python molurus bivittatus, with her hatching eggs. Photo by Burkhard Kahl.

Sexing snakes by external characters is difficult but not always impossible. As a general rule, male snakes (bottom) have a thicker tail base to house the hemipenes and a relatively longer tail. Females (top) have the taper of the tail uniform, not enlarged at the base, and have the overall length of the tail less (often greatly less) than in the male. Photo: J. Gee.

habitat of the species concerned is essential if any degree of breeding success is to be achieved.

DETERMINATION OF SEXES

Perhaps the most obvious requirement for captive breeding is a male and a female of the species to be bred; in other words, a true pair. It is not immediately easy to sex boid species, particularly young specimens. In adults it is usually the case that the

males are shorter and slimmer than the females. A 3 m (10 ft) example of a male Indian Python, for example, is a large one, whereas a 5 m (15 ft +) female is not unusual. As a method of sex determination, however, this is not very reliable. In some species the male's tail is longer and more gently tapered than that of the female. There may be a bulge on either side of the tail base where the inverted hemipenes are situated. The male

The cloacal spurs of a boid look something like dog claws but actually represent the last phalanx of a vestigial foot. Male snakes commonly have larger and more mobile spurs than females of the same species. Photo of *Epicrates striatus*: J. Dodd.

may have a greater number of paired subcaudal (below the tail) scales. The "claw" vestiges of the hind limbs (cloacal spurs) may be larger and more prominent in the males than in the females. In spite of the number of these apparent differences, none of them is a really reliable method of sex determination.

The most efficient method of sex determination in the boids is the process known as probing. In normal circumstances, the male hemipenes (the two halves of a divided penis) are inverted into deep pockets at either side of the vent in the tail base. If a probe is inserted carefully inside the inverted hemipenis, it may be gently pushed

This somewhat diagrammatic drawing shows the position of the cloacal spurs just to the side and slightly anterior to the anal plate covering the vent. Only the pointed to blunt tip may be visible in some species, especially in females.

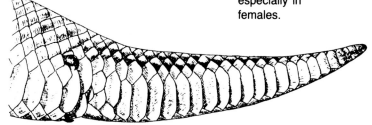

A family group of Green Tree Pythons, *Chondropython viridis*. The young are hatched a vivid orange to brownish color and soon become distinctly yellowish. As the yellow young grow and mature the color gradually becomes more greenish until the bright green of the adult is assumed. In most snakes green is a composite color consisting of a yellow overlay on a bluish background. If the yellow is reduced or absent, blue specimens result; blue Green Tree Pythons are not uncommon. Photo: L. Porras.

"Probing is considered a dangerous procedure, and amateurs probably should not attempt it until they have seen it performed by an experienced hand."

some distance (usually the equivalent of about 10 subcaudal scales) in the direction of the tail tip. In females it usually is impossible to push the probe more than the width of one or two subcaudals. Probes may be purchased from specialist suppliers in various sizes. They usually are made of stainless steel or synthetic material and have a smooth, spherical tip. The tip should be lubricated with a little petroleum jelly before sexing is attempted. Select an appropriate size probe and probe gently and firmly, but never force it, as it may injure the snake. Probing is considered a dangerous procedure, and amateurs probably should not attempt it until they have seen it performed by an experienced hand.

BREEDING CYCLES

The breeding cycles of boids are affected by environmental and seasonal changes. It is thought that most wild boids breed once per year when the weather is suitable. Breeding condition may be brought on by seasonal changes in day length (photoperiod), by increases in temperature, and/or by changes in humidity (rainy season). It is very important to be familiar with the natural biotope of the species in question. The provision of appropriate seasonal changes in the terrarium will greatly increase the possibility of captive breeding.

COURTSHIP

Most species of boids are fairly solitary outside of the breeding season and would normally ignore chance meetings with members of their own or opposite sexes. During the breeding season the female snake, especially after molting, releases a pheromone (vitellogenin) on the surface of the skin from areas between the scales. This pheromone attracts the males and appears to have aphrodisiac properties on them. In the wild, several males may be attracted to a sexually active female, and minor wrestling matches and displays of strength will ensue to vie for the right to mate with her.

The most likely way of getting breeding results with most species is to keep the sexes separate for most of the year. Then, when a female is in breeding condition (brought on by the appropriate climatic changes) and has just molted, introduce two or three males to her in her terrarium. Combat rituals should then take place, and the most dominant male will court and copulate with the female.

Courtship consists of the

"The most likely way of getting breeding results with most species is to keep the sexes separate for most of the year."

Snakes lay eggs that seem large compared to the girth of the mother. This Bull Snake is depositing an egg almost equal to the maximum girth and will follow it with a dozen or more eggs of similar size. The eggs of pythons tend to be quite elongated. Photo: W. B. Allen, Jr.

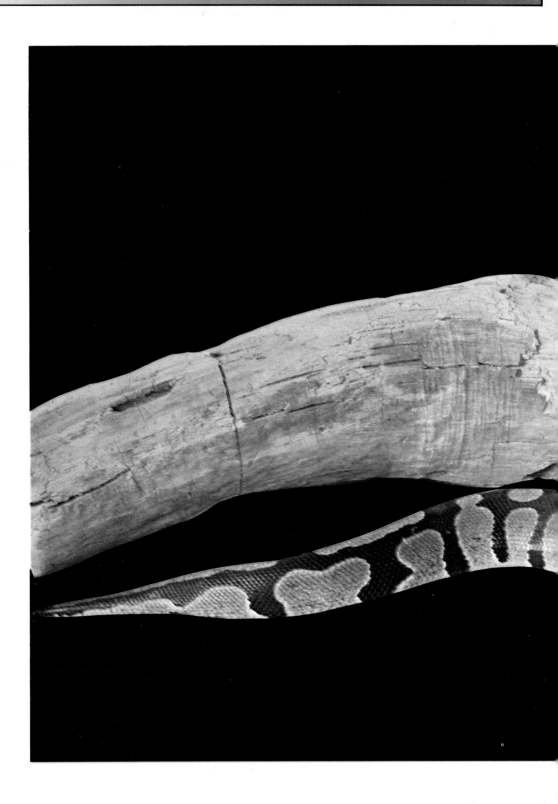

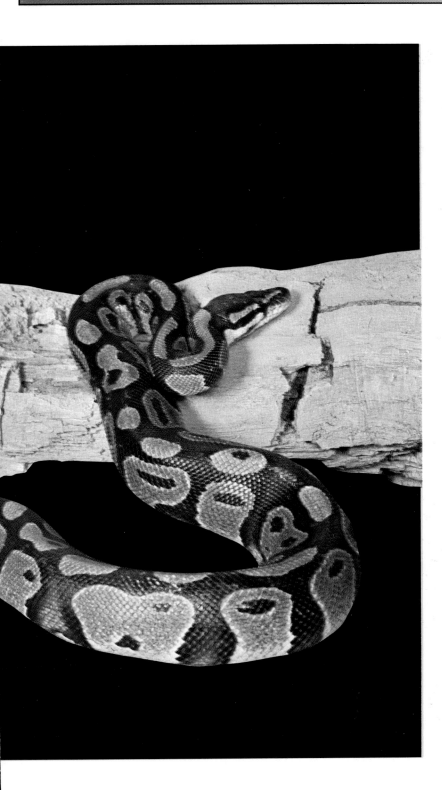

The Ball Python,
Python regius.
Photo by J. Dodd.

male crawling over the female in short, jerky movements while continually "tasting" her body with his tongue. When he reaches the appropriate position along the female's body, he will attempt to push his tail under hers and stimulate her cloacal region by scratching with his "spurs." If the female is receptive, she will lift her tail and open the lips of her cloaca so that the male is able to insert one of his now everted hemipenes. Copulation may last from a few minutes to several hours; there appears to be no major activity during copulation itself, and the fertilizing sperm enter the female's body passively. After copulation is over the males should be moved back to their separate cages and the female preferably left in her own.

GRAVID FEMALES

A female snake containing fertilized eggs is known as a gravid female. In the family Boidae there are species that are oviparous and those that are ovoviviparous. The former (including all of the Pythoninae) lay white eggs with a parchment-like shell; these are usually "incubated" by the female until they hatch. The ovoviviparous species (virtually all the boas and remaining species of the family) give birth to live young after they have developed to full-term within the eggs in the female's body. In simple terms, it can be said that pythons are egg-layers and boas are live-bearers (although there may be some exceptions in the latter case).

The period from copulation to oviposition or birth varies from species to species and depends to some extent on prevailing temperatures. In the Indian Python it takes about 60 days from fertilization to egg-laying; in the Common Boa, about 100 days from fertilization to birth. At an advanced stage of gravidity the females take on a plump appearance and the eggs can usually be discerned as bulges along the posterior part of the body. At this stage the snake may refuse all food until

after egg-laying or birth. This is no cause for concern as it appears to be quite natural behavior, probably so that the already heavy snake is not weighed down by a heavy food item should the necessity to flee from predators arise. It is best not to handle gravid females more than is absolutely necessary, as undue disturbance may jeopardize the satisfactory development of the embryos. It is essential that optimum temperatures are available in the terrarium during the period of gravidity. Excessively low temperatures may kill or seriously affect the development of the young.

EGG-LAYING

Most members of the subfamily Pythoninae are known to incubate their eggs, while it is suspected in others. The female seeks out a secluded, suitable spot where the correct temperatures and humidity seem to be the major factors in satisfactory development

A hatching group of d'Albert's Pythons, *Liasis albertisii*. The young do not all emerge at the same time, with some young being "afraid" to leave the egg for hours or even days after the rest of the brood emerge. The young snakes will not eat until after the first shed. Photo: C. Banks.

The Blood Python, *Python curtus brongersmai*. *Photo by P. J. Stafford.*

"Pythons (at least some species) are unique among snakes in being able to incubate their eggs with elevated female body temperatures."

This female Burmese Python, *Python molurus bivittatus*, incubates and guards the developing eggs and stays with the brood until hatching is complete. As a general rule, adult pythons and boas do not eat their young, at least not immediately after birth or hatching...but it is best to separate adults and young to be on the safe side. Photo: B. Kahl.

of the embryos. In the wild, a female will have many prospective egg-laying sites, and a few days before oviposition she will start searching for her ideal spot. In the terrarium a female python will become extremely restless at this time, continually crawling around the relatively small space. At this time she must be disturbed as little as possible. Some females seem to be unable to find a satisfactory egg-laying site in the terrarium and end up scattering the eggs all over the place; in such cases she will show only partial parental care and the eggs must be removed for artificial incubation. In most cases, however, the eggs are laid in a cone-shaped stack on the substrate and the snake coils around them, covering them up completely with her body.

Pythons (at least some species) are unique among snakes in being able to incubate their eggs with elevated female body temperatures. During incubation the female's body muscles twitch; the lower the temperature, the more often she will twitch. These muscular spasms are related to the snake's ability to raise her body temperature as much as 7°C (12-13°F) above that of

the surrounding environment, this producing a suitable incubation temperature for her eggs.

The best captive breeding results seem to occur when the female python is allowed to incubate her own eggs; she obviously has more evolutionary experience for it than we do! The eggs are sticky when laid and tend to adhere to each other quite tightly; you should not attempt to separate the eggs, as the shells may be damaged. If the female snake appears to be incubating her eggs naturally, it is best to leave well enough alone and allow things to take their own course.

Maintain a terrarium temperature of around 27°C (81°F) at this time reduced by about 5°C (9°F) at night. The female and her egg stack should be sprayed daily with lukewarm water to maintain the humidity. During incubation some of the eggs may start to turn most unhealthy looking colors and mold may appear on them. These are either infertile eggs or those in which the embryo has died in the shell. These should not be removed unless they are pushed outside the stack. The presence of rotting eggs in the stack does not seem to affect the normal development of the healthy eggs, and in fact

"The presence of rotting eggs in the stack does not seem to affect the normal development of the healthy eggs, and in fact they may well aid development."

they may well aid development.

During incubation the female will not feed and may only occasionally leave the egg stack at night to drink. After about 60 days the eggs will start hatching. As soon as this occurs the female will leave the stack and show no further interest in her young, which are fully independent little pythons.

BIRTH

Most boas are ovoviviparous or live-bearing. There does not seem to be any preference of sites for a female boa to give birth; she will drop her young anywhere and shows no parental care. The young may still be enclosed in a transparent membrane-like sac (the egg "shell" in ovo-viviparous species) but will escape from this shortly after birth. Sometimes a few infertile or only partially developed eggs may be included in the litter; these are useless and must be discarded. Ensure that there is a high humidity in the terrarium at such a time so the membranes do not dry out too rapidly and adhere to the little

This hatchling *Python molurus bivittatus* shows a pattern identical to that of the adult. Note the straight cut through the adjoining egg shell produced by the egg tooth, a sharp-edged "pimple" on the snout of fully developed young. The egg tooth is lost within hours of hatching and is never conspicuous. Photo: B. Kahl.

snakes, giving them problems. Juvenile snakes with dried out membranes attached to them should be gently sprayed with lukewarm water at intervals until the snake is able to free itself. Sometimes a little careful help may be given, but on no account should you attempt to remove the yolk sac, which will still be attached about mid-way under the abdomen. This will come away in its own time. It is best to remove young snakes from the parental cage for separate rearing.

ARTIFICIAL INCUBATION

Some egg-laying pythons may abandon their eggs; these may be removed for artificial incubation. A simple incubator can be made with a small terrarium containing a light bulb (preferably a red or blue one to minimize the light) controlled with a thermostat to maintain the internal temperature of the incubator at 28-31°C (82-88°F). This may be reduced by about 5°C (9°F) at night, but it does not appear to be strictly necessary. The eggs are placed in a tray on an absorbent, sterile substance such as vermiculite which has been mixed with an equal volume of water. This substrate should be moist but not wet. The eggs may be covered with a clean, damp, preferably cotton, cloth (terry towelling is ideal) or paper towels, which should be changed at regular intervals. The whole tray is placed in the incubator. The eggs should not be turned as one would do with birds' eggs; they should stay in the same position all of the time. If you pick eggs up for examination, be sure to replace them in exactly the same position. The eggs should be examined daily and misted sparingly with lukewarm water.

As the eggs develop they will absorb water and become taut-shelled. After a time it may be possible to make out blood vessels of the developing embryos through the shell. The eggs should hatch in about 60 days (hatching may be slower, so don't give up until the eggs are obviously rotten). The fully developed embryo

"It is best to remove young snakes from the parental cage for separate rearing."

"The eggs should not be turned as one would do with birds' eggs; they should stay in the same position all of the time."

absorbing the remaining contents of the yolk sac, as well as developing the use of the lung(s).

REARING

Young boids are relatively easy to rear when compared with other species of snake. Most hatchlings or newly born young are capable of taking at least baby mice, and some of the larger species can take a fully grown mouse at their first meal. Hatchling snakes do not normally feed until after their first molt, which is normally two to eight days after hatching. It is preferable to rear juvenile boids in small containers with the minimum of decorations, at least for the first few weeks. Juvenile snakes should be handled regularly in order to tame them. If tamed at an early age, even the larger, more aggressive species will remain docile for the rest of their lives.

Snake eggs can be incubated in any suitable container that will retain the proper moisture levels. The choice of incubation substrate varies from keeper to keeper, although both vermiculite and damp paper towels are commonly recommended. Mold and drying are the main problems encountered if the temperature is maintained at the proper temperature for the species. Photo: W. B. Allen, Jr.

snake has a sharp "egg-tooth" on the snout, with which it slits open the shell. The egg-tooth is shed shortly after hatching. Young pythons often seem to be in no particular hurry to leave the egg after they start to hatch, and they may spend a couple of days with just the head sticking out, drawing themselves quickly back into the shell if disturbed. It is a great temptation to "help" babies that appear to be taking a long time to hatch, but remember that this is a natural process that is best left to the snakes; by "helping" we may do more harm than good. The hatchlings are

Suggested Reading

Breeding Terrarium Animals
Elke Zimmermann
ISBN 0-86622-182-4
TFH H-1078
384 pages; 175 color photos; numerous line drawings.
   The best book available on captive breeding of herps, including commonly kept snake species, both native and exotic. Must reading for the serious hobbyist. Moderately technical.

Beginning With Snakes
Richard F. Stratton
ISBN 0-87666-934-8
TFH KW-127
96 pages; 52 color photos 22 B & W photos
   Basic introduction to snake care. Non technical.

Boas and Other Non-venomous Snakes
Werner Frank
ISBN 0-87666-922-4
TFH KW-002
96 pages; 27 color photos; 53 B & W photos
   Good introduction to captive snakes, with emphasis on diseases and easy to keep species. Non-technical.

Kingsnakes and Milk Snakes
Robert Markel
ISBN 0-86622-664-8
TFH TS-125
   Audience; A comprehensive coverage of all the species and subspecies of kinsnakes and milk snakes, genus *Lampropeltis*. All four dozen taxa (and many variants) are described in detail and illustrated in full color by specially-drawn color diagrams. Nearly all the subspecies are also illustrated in color photographs. Special sections on husbandry cover breeding and feeding problems. Maps. High school and above.

Snakes as Pets
Dr. Hobart M. Smith
ISBN 0-87666-908-9
TFH AP-925
160 pages; 51 color photos; 55 B & W photos
   A standard reference by a prominent American herpetologist on collecting and keeping North American snakes as pets; heavily illustrated, with many western species. Non-technical.

THE COMPLETELY ILLUSTRATED ATLAS OF REPTILES AND AMPHIBIANS FOR THE TERRARIUM
Fritz Jürgen Obst,
Dr. Klaus Richter,
Dr. Udo Jacob
ISBN 0-86622-958-2
TFH H-1102
Here is a truly comprehensive and beautiful volume covering all the reptiles and amphibians kept in terrariums plus virtually all the oddballs and rarities any hobbyist (or scientist, for that matter) is likely to ever see or want to know about. Illustrated in full color are hundreds of common and rare reptiles and amphibians, invertebrates, food animals, terrarium plants, environments, and diseases, with hundreds more black and white photos and line drawings. But don't think that this book is just pictures—the authoritataive and useful text covers thousands of species, the majority of genera, and hundreds of topics dealing with terrarium care and natural history. The alphabetical arrangement makes it easy to find information on almost any topic you can think of, and you can be sure the information is correct and up-to-date.

Encyclopedia of Reptiles and Amphibians
John F. Breen
ISBN 0-87666-220-3
TFH H-935
576 pages; 267 colors; 316 B & W photos
Fine introduction to the world of living herps. Covers both native and exotic snakes in detail, with information on natural history of most species commonly kept in captivity. Section on feeding live foods. Non-technical.

Pythons and Boas
Peter J. Stafford
ISBN 0-86622-183-2
TFH PS-846
192 pages; 111 color photos; 22 B & W photos plus numerous line drawings
The best coverage of the popular pythons and boas. Must reading for every hobbyist with even a passing interest in the group. Excellent natural history and care sections, with many species (common and uncommon) illustrated in color. Moderately technical.

Index

Page numbers in **bold** refer to photographs.

BOAS & PYTHONS
AND OTHER FRIENDLY SNAKES
BY JOHN COBORN